PASSAGE
THROUGH
MID-LIFE

Fellow Pilgrims rejoice! At last someone has provided us with a map for our "road less traveled." Thank you Fr. Robb.
—Dr. Timothy C. Hoffman, Founding Director, Ambrosian Associates in Pastoral Counseling

A profound and reassuring description of the hardest journey of all, our inner journey, this book is a "must read," especially for those in the second half of life. Paul's approach is to walk with us, not talk at us.
—Dick Wright, Ph.D., consultant, Wright Directions Consulting Firm

Paul Robb's insightful exploration of the dynamics of continuing personal conversion serves as a timely reminder to me to more consciously allow that "inward spiral moving ever more deeply into the center of (my) being" where God/my true self is to be found.
—Gabrielle Morgan, P.B.V.M.

Equipped with the tools of theology, psychology and his own life experience, Paul Robb finds in the scriptures and the life of Jesus the rationale for life's crises. "Suffering is a means that God uses to help us know ourselves."
—Anthony Brodniak, M.M.

This detailed study of the spiritual journey is most welcome in this age which seeks quick spiritual cures. Robb contributes much to our understanding and to living incarnational spirituality.
—Virginia L. Sampson, S.U.S.C.

PASSAGE
THROUGH
MID-LIFE

A SPIRITUAL
JOURNEY
TO
WHOLENESS

PAUL ROBB

ave maria press AmP Notre Dame, Indiana

www.avemariapress.com
International Standard Book Number: 1-59471-051-1
Cover and text design by John Carson
Cover photo © Corbis
Printed and bound in the United States of America.
Library of Congress Cataloging-in-Publication Data is available.

CONTENTS

PREFACE

The origins of these reflections on our mid-life journey began over thirty-five years ago when I was asked to guide some young people who wanted to know about the spiritual life. The spirit of the Second Vatican Council challenged us to find new ways as well as to return to our origins. Even though it called for a study of beginnings, it was not a time for turning back to old ways. Old ways were being cracked open. It was a time filled with promise and excitement. For us Jesuits it was a time for rediscovering the *Spiritual Exercises* of Saint Ignatius Loyola. Individually directed retreats with their emphasis on affections and spiritual direction became again a source for spiritual renewal.

I found myself thrust into the midst of this heady rejuvenation. When I tried to articulate what we were trying to accomplish by spiritual direction, I found myself uneasy with many common statements. "Faith growth," "increase in prayer life," "growing closer to God," all seemed highly desirous but were a bit nebulous to me. They didn't point out a way to these lofty goals. In searching for my way I was moved by the words of Jesus telling us how God works. He told Nicodemus in John 3 that a person must be born again or, as he explained to the apostles in John 12:24, that a seed had to die in order to come to a full harvest. The images of death and birth do not deal with just ordinary changes or transitions, they portray radical events. The dynamics of our entering into life and leaving it have their own particular qualities and finality.

I began to see spiritual direction as aiding people to come to know themselves through the dying and birthing that occur in our daily lives. Saint Augustine exclaims "Let me know myself Lord so I can know you." With confidence that in knowing ourselves we come to know God, I found that it is by living and growing through these fearful experiences of death and rebirth that we grow in faith and in our relationship with God. We also grow in our relationship with ourselves and with others. Jesus, in his dialog with Nicodemus, tells how it is with someone born again. He says, "You must be born from above. The wind [spirit] blows wherever it pleases; you hear its sound but you cannot tell where it comes from or where it is going. That is how it is with all who are born of the Spirit" (Jn 3:7–8). We feel moved from within but we don't know what it means.

Finally arriving at this articulation that seemed to satisfy, I found that it was not the end of my exploration but another beginning. Around this time I read Elisabeth Kübler-Ross's book *On Death and Dying*. I recognized that we go through the dynamics she articulates almost daily when we are blocked or disappointed. They weave together our lives from the beginning to the end. We can see them in an infant who is beginning to learn to walk and talk. We can see them in ordinary setbacks, but they are more evident and forceful when we experience transitions and more significant frustration of our plans. This insightful discovery changed the way I looked at spirituality. Instead of trying to find ways and practices in which to deny myself so that I could die and be reborn, I began to look for the ways that this dying happened in my daily life as well as at more significant times of change. This changed view has many drastic implications. When we adopt practices of self-denial, we continue to be in charge of our lives. Even though the practices may be hard, we can get some satisfaction that we are *doing* something (for God?). I became aware of how often we avoid situations when we will be blocked and thwarted. We strive to avoid shame, being humiliated, appearing a loser. But when we accept these situations as opportunities to experience a spiritual rebirth, the tables are turned upside down. I found that when the trials come, they are more salutary while being more painful.

Some years after my initial foray into the world of spirituality, I had a second learning experience. In 1973 I began the Institute for Spiritual Leadership to educate spiritual directors. Two realities became clear with this development. My first learning occurred when I read the book *Psychosynthesis* by Roberto Assagioli. an Italian psychiatrist. What struck me most was that he emphasized that there are stages in the process of spiritual development. The path was marked by hardships and challenges as well as breakthrough graces that brought new life. He wrote that it is "a long and arduous journey an adventure through strange lands full of surprises, difficulties and even dangers." I visited Professor Assagioli in Italy a short time before his death. I thanked him for putting stress on synthesis and integration rather than analysis and breaking down. He was writing about life, and life in abundance.

With the light of this understanding of process, I began to see spiritual growth and spiritual direction in a new and wider perspective. It appeared as an inward spiral moving ever more deeply into the center of our being. Each phase was highlighted by the fearful dynamics of dying to be reborn. I began to see similar phases articulated in scripture, the fathers of the church, and the mystics. Saint Paul's prayer in Ephesians that our hidden self would grow strong so that Christ may live in our hearts through faith became for me the bedrock of a spirituality of development and process. Paul helped me to focus on the hidden, the True Self, that is often masked by our false self. Perhaps the phases stand out more clearly in John of the Cross' experience when he writes of the different characteristics and dynamics of the Dark Night of Senses and Dark Night of Spirit.

My second learning was on a more concrete and personal level. It came through and with the men and women who participated in the nine-month program of the Institute for Spiritual Leadership. Most of the participants at the Institute were middle-aged and older. They ranged in age from over thirty to over seventy. They were Catholic and non-Catholic, religious, married, and lay persons. These men and women came from all parts of the world and brought the riches and insights of their native countries. They brought their life experiences of successes and failures. They knew something of the deaths and rebirths that Jesus talked about. In my classes they found words for their experiences, thereby bringing them more clearly to light. By naming them they could integrate, rather than reject, negative experiences.

One person in the very first program stands out. She was a seventy-year-old woman religious who had been a provincial superior in her congregation. When asked before the whole group why she came to the program, she replied "I've come to grow." Her awareness of herself and her attitude marked the qualities most common in all who came. Her statement helped me to solidify the most helpful quality we looked for in applicants to the program. We looked for men and women who had some degree of self-knowledge and a desire to grow. We were alert to how much they were tested and tempted in their lives, believing the statement in Hebrews 2 that Jesus became our compassionate high priest because he had been tempted much.

Given this quality of participants, it was a joy to aid in their spiritual growth and development that would be the best foundation of their own future work. Besides my nine-month course on the dynamics and process of conversion, we also stressed creative ways to address and listen to one's own interior. Both of these contributed to the participants' growing self-knowledge and a level of sharing that issued from deep respect for each one's process on the spiritual journey. We found that cultural differences took second place to the basic humanness of each person. The deep reverence and respect that marked the Institute aided in each one's confronting his or her life creatively and in companionship. What may have been hidden for years could be uncovered, admitted, and celebrated. A strong sense of community grew naturally.

These remarks would be empty if I did not express my deep gratitude to God for sending Suzanne Zuercher, O.S.B., to the Institute in its early years. More than any other she grasped the spirit of what I was trying to do. She contributed to it and expanded its dynamics to such an extent that she became like a co-founder of the Institute. Besides developing creative ways of dealing with the interior, she contributed to the overall sense of reverence and respect. For me personally she has been a faithful companion and friend.

I address this work to all men and women who hear and are challenged by the Spirit breathing a new fire throughout the world. This fire was partly inflamed by the Spirit found in the decrees of Vatican Council II. This same fire of the Spirit burns in men and women from every corner of the world. Descriptions of their journeys are similar despite great differences in language and customs. Such people search for a mature spirituality that resonates with their life experiences. I address all people of goodwill who desire greater freedom in faith and justice, deeper life in the Spirit, and a love more free from fear. I also write for those who seek spiritual renewal and find themselves lost in a very unfamiliar land of darkness and light.

Lastly, and most importantly, I write for those who may be experiencing in themselves the confusion and chaos that are part of the conversion journey. I write for those who are bewildered at their own and others' experience. After many years of prayer and faithful service, why should strong doubts arise, intense passions flame, meaning and truths grow stale, questions abound, and new kinds of darkness and sterility touch so deeply? The love of God that once sustained and motivated now seems elusive and illusory. Even a stubborn, sincere, and willful "I believe" brings no solace or respite. In fact, it can echo mockingly. Darkness replaces light, and depression becomes a familiar, though unwelcome, companion. The words of Psalm 88 rise bitterly to our lips: "Now darkness is my one companion left." Life becomes a desert similar to that described by T. S. Eliot in *The Waste Land*:

What are the roots that clutch, what branches
   grow
Out of this stony rubbish? Son of man,
You cannot say, or guess, for you know only
A heap of broken images, where the sun
sears,
And the dead trees give no shelter, the cricket
   no relief,
And the dry stone no sound of water.

INTRODUCTION

Mid-Life: A Seed Must Die

Why another book on mid-life, you may ask? The crises of mid-life have been described and explored. Psychologists have analyzed them. They have been sensationalized by novelists. A number of books describe the many changes taking place in our bodies at this time and prescribe remedies for better health and a longer life. They look on mid-life as the herald of the inevitable process of aging. Amid all the publicity, we, especially those of us who do not feel we are in a crisis, might ignore the more important but subtle changes that take place in our spirits. At mid-life, whether we experience a crisis or not, we are invited to spiritual growth and life in abundance.

I write this book on mid-life from another perspective that may help us to consider our lives in a deeper and broader context. Mid-life does not signal the lessening and end of life, but the expansion of life. Paying attention to what our spirits are telling us provides us with a fuller perspective to make mid-life a time of growth. This spiritual dimension puts our experiences into a new and broader context. These experiences are common to men and women in all cultures. They help us to understand our forefathers, and we will pass our newfound wisdom on to future generations.

Carl Jung intimates that all mid-life crises are spiritual crises. He suggests that at mid-life we are called to confront ourselves. For everyone this is a demanding challenge, but for some it becomes a crisis. He writes:

> The afternoon of life must have a significance of its own and cannot be merely a pitiful appendage to life's morning. For an aging person it is a duty and a necessity to give serious attention to himself. Instead of doing this many older people prefer to be hypochondriacs, niggards, doctrinaires, applauders of the past or eternal adolescents—all lamentable substitutes? for the illumination of the self. We need colleges for forty year olds to prepare them for their coming life. Our religions were always such schools in the past, but how many people regard them as such today (pp. 108–9).

The Institute for Spiritual Leadership, which I founded in 1972, became such a college to help mid-lifers navigate the deep seas of life. It fostered spiritual maturity during the mid-life journey. This book treats of a spirituality that meets the needs of those in the second half of life.

A growing sense that something is missing in our lives, a feeling of emptiness, announces the arrival of mid-life. We may judge that life's adventure is over and all we need do is to enjoy retirement. Our spirit intimates otherwise, calling us to live more congruently with our interior and our hidden Self. We experience a call for something more fulfilling. We look for deeper meaning that resonates with an inner need and desire. We desire to live in a way that is more personally meaningful and satisfying. New feelings and emotions begin to flood us. Memories that demand our attention emerge from our forgotten past. Those parts of ourselves that we have repressed or ignored begin to stir and seek expression in our lives; they will not be denied. Regrets over missed opportunities may haunt us. Personal questions of faith and meaning lead us to explore our hearts. We need to find something new within ourselves rather than searching outside ourselves.

This is how we experience our call to journey to our inner depths where we find our Self and God, and renewed relationships with our neighbors. Sam Keen illustrates this call for something more and reveals the reasons why we might consider it a crisis.

> Something calls us to break out of our shell,
> to abandon our cocoons, to leave the security
> of personality-position-prestige and begin
> the solitary journey to the center of the self.
> Before us opens a new path into an unknown
> future, excitement, and terror. If we choose to
> go on that journey, as Dante said, "midway in
> life we enter a dark wood"; or, as the mystics
> said, we go into the dark night of the soul
> (p. 123).

Sam Keen encourages us to accept the invitation to endure our mid-life passage. He reminds us that those who have made the journey before will inspire us. "Those who decide to undertake what has always been recognized as the heroic journey into the heart of the self will have many ancient heroes and heroines as guides" (p. 126). We may be moved by the writings of other contemporaries like Pierre Teilhard de Chardin, Thomas Merton, or Henri Nouwen. Many current searchers and humanistic psychologists, who look for a fuller, more meaningful life, add insights to our discoveries.

The journey that Keen alludes to is called affective conversion. Affective conversion plunges us onto the path during which we "lose our lives" in order "to be born of the spirit." In the gospel of John, Jesus advised Nicodemus that life in the Spirit is like being blown by the wind. "The wind blows where it pleases; you can hear its sound, but you cannot tell where it comes from or where it is going. So it is with everyone who is born of the Spirit" (Jn 3:8). Affective conversion brings about changes on all levels of our person. It touches our way of being present through seeing and hearing, our way of relating with others with our affections, and our way of choosing to live and be in the world.

We find the invitation to affective conversion primarily in the scriptures. We find our heroes in the patriarchs and prophets of the Hebrew scriptures. We find it in the apostles who accepted Jesus' invitation to find life in abundance. The fathers of the church and the mystics have told us of their experience of the journey of conversion. From these and other sources we find help to give understanding to our experience. We find the reality of what Jeremiah advises: "Set up signposts, raise landmarks; mark the road well, the way by which you went. Come home, come home to these towns of yours. How long will you hesitate? For Yahweh is creating something new on earth" (Jer 31:21–22).

In addition to heightened emotions and feeling, affective conversion also begins a journey that takes place over time. It initiates changes that lead us ever deeper into the recesses of ourselves. It impels us to work through stages of dryness, of darkness and light, of consolation and desolation. It enables our "hidden self" to grow strong as Saint Paul prays.

> May he [the Father] give you the power
> through his Spirit for your hidden self to
> grow strong, so that Christ may live in your
> hearts through faith, and then, planted in
> love and built on love, you will with all the
> saints have strength to grasp the breadth and
> the length, the height and the depth; until,
> knowing the love of Christ, which is beyond
> on knowledge, you are filled with the utter
> fullness of God (Eph 3:16–19).

In the conclusion of his prayer, Saint Paul praises the Father "whose power, working in us, can do infinitely more than we can ask or imagine." He intimates that affective conversion begins with God and not with us. The power of the Father works in us. He asks for our cooperation, not our initiative. We are invited to enter God's school. The fathers of the church and the mystics have outlined the progression by which God usually teaches in this school. Knowing the "lesson plan," they indicate how we can cooperate in responding to the Father's initiative. I plan to treat the stages of the journey in subsequent books while I concentrate in this book on our affections, the feelings, and emotions that instigate our affective conversion.

Our affections, like the wind, are our first manifestation of changes ready to take place in our life. Our mid-life passage involves feelings and emotions that shake our daily lives. They are confusing. They lift us up as well as bring us down into the pits. They put our way of living into jeopardy. Even more, we sense that they touch the roots of our lives. They reach deep into our being, our personality, our choices, our history, our very Self. They touch places in us that are unknown, where we are strangers to ourselves.

It is difficult to endure affective conversion. Miriam Greenspan knows from experience about the fear and difficulties that arise when our emotions and feelings, especially the negative ones, erupt. She writes:

> Seething emotions pollute our psychological, moral, and spiritual environment. . . . Emotional illiteracy has less to do with our inability to subdue negative emotions than it does with our inability to authentically and mindfully *feel* them. What looks like a problem with emotional control actually has its source in a widespread ignorance about how to tolerate painful emotional energies and use these energies for emotional, spiritual, and social transformation (p. xii).

Peter Faber, a companion of Ignatius Loyola and a well-known master of the life of the Spirit, highlighted the importance of our affections. He wrote that if you wanted to know where the Spirit is in a person's life you should help him to know his feelings and emotions. The chancellor of the Archdiocese of Mainz, whom Peter was counseling, wrote to Ignatius Loyola asking him to send more men who were "Masters of the Affections" in the spiritual life.

We still find this need for "masters of the affections." They will help us to know who we are and where God's spirit is calling us. Greenspan's book is a practical guide to help us avoid suppressing and diverting our emotions so we can live them and learn their wisdom. Learning the wisdom of our affections will help us to realize the fruits of Saint Paul's prayer. In his letter to the Ephesians, Paul prays: "May the eyes of our heart be enlightened, that you may know what is the hope that belong to his call" (Eph 1:3).

At mid-life we are at a point of decision. We must decide whether we will accept or refuse this invitation to grow into greater intimacy with God, with ourselves, and with others. If we accept the invitation to this fearful journey, our familiar security will be uprooted. We will have to change. Columnist Sydney Harris, in an editorial on Thomas Merton whom he considered to be a man who continued to grow, observes that most of us will refuse this call to intimacy.

> We are meant to change as we accumulate years and experience, but most of us seem to change (when we do) not for the better but for the worse. Age seems to bring not only hardening of the physical arteries, but a hardening of the mental and spiritual arteries as well. . . . The whole part of "growth" is acquiring a wider angle of vision, not a narrower one, of opening one's sensibilities, not closing them. Whatever your views were at the age of 30 or 50, if they have not changed and expanded, not contracted, you have failed to fulfill your potential as a human being. Most of us never succeed in outgrowing the imprint of our early environment: we simply become more of what we were at the start of life's journey (*Chicago Sun-Times*).

To begin a journey into an unfamiliar, haunting land is frightening, but not to know whether we will find life or death, blessing or curse, at the end can be terrifying. But to enter that journey, even with all its uncertainties, provides the possibility of finding life, and life in abundance. Not to begin the journey, but instead to harden and steel oneself against it, is already death.

With the light of scripture, the mystics, and modern writers, I propose to be a spiritual companion who will walk with you on the journey. We can endure the deserts and not be sidetracked during the times of relief. Knowing the dynamic inner movements and finding words for our experience can help us feel that we are not alone. This knowledge does not exempt us from the pain and suffering of our particular journey. It does not tell us which path to follow. Above all it must not interfere with the Spirit of Jesus who leads each of us in our unique way. It can help us, however, not to be afraid of our fear. Fear of our fear paralyzes us into its own paranoia. Jesus tells us not to be afraid and assures us that he will be with us. I believe he means that we should not be afraid of our fear. Healthy fear focuses us keenly, like a mountain climber, on the next step to take, the next hold to grasp. This is the fear that allows climbers to scale higher heights. It does not paralyze them.

In this book I will focus on the feelings and emotions that mark our mid-life passage. Reflecting on the times in my life when I felt I was losing my grip on my life, I was reminded of Jesus' admonition that a seed must die in order to live and bring forth good fruit. Then I read Elisabeth Kübler-Ross's book *On Death and Dying*. Her articulation of the progressive feelings and emotions that a dying person suffers provides a vehicle to understand Jesus' advice to those of us who are at mid-life.

This cycle of feelings and emotions is well-known to us. It enters our lives from the beginning when we learn to walk and talk. After hearing of these dynamics in class, a young mother observed and documented their progression from denial to final acceptance in her young son when she refused to let one of his playmates stay overnight. Not believing her refusal, he got angry and told her she did not love him. Then, bargaining for his case, he cajoled her with promises of what he would do for the family. After her final refusal he became silent and sad. Later still he recovered and found new energy and life.

At mid-life, we may experience these same dynamics more intensely. By naming them and bringing them to consciousness, we may cooperate with the power of the Spirit who calls us to maturity and the fullness of life. My focus and intent in this book is to explore the feelings and emotions we go through in losing our lives so our hidden selves can grow strong and Christ may live in our hearts. Our fear may be lessened.

I begin my reflections by looking at Jesus of Nazareth who revealed in his own life the fullness of the journey to life. He experienced all the feelings and emotions that we experience. He was angry, anxious, and sad. His affective life inspires me to write this book. In Chapter 2, I show that the kingdom of God is to be found within us. The book of Deuteronomy tells us that we find God "on our lips and in our hearts." Saint Paul tells us that we find Jesus, the Lord, in the same way. In Chapter 3, I consider the disillusionment and confusion that are the onset of our mid-life passage and conversion. Kübler-Ross documents the denial that accompanies the feeling of confusion and frustration at our lives being interrupted. We are stopped and forced to walk another road.

In Chapter 4, I treat the reactive anger that arises when we feel powerless. We can do nothing to stop the invading disease of meaninglessness. Chapter 5 considers our growing anxiety that becomes obvious by our attempts at making promises, bargaining, to alleviate the pain. Our frequent attempts to plot and plan seem to initiate a vicious circle. Then, worn out by these feelings and frustrated by the burden of realizing there is no escape, we are led to growing helplessness and depression. While still in this sadness and lamentation of our condition, we move on to Chapter 6 that promises to shed light on our suffering. We begin to understand the value and meaning of suffering in our lives. Unexpectedly and remarkably, at that point, we find we are ready to let go of our lives as they have been. We have the energy to accept and choose this new life being offered.

I then insert Chapter 7 on hope. Dr. Kübler-Ross suggests that hope springs up in the most unusual ways and in many unexpected places, helping us to recognize hope as it is rather than as we imagine it to be. This provides a new glimpse of hope and ways of recognizing and appreciating signs of hope among those who seem condemned. We find hope in our dying. In Chapter 8, I consider how and where these "death and dying" experiences are leading us. They lead us to our hidden selves where with all the saints we can know "the length and breadth, height and depth of the love of God."

Jesus' example has inspired me and I write in gratitude for his many gifts to me. When he reiterated his Father's command to choose life, he addressed all men and women, but middle-agers in a special way. He announced that he had come to bring life. He encouraged us to choose life and to continue to grow. He promised an abundance of life to those who listened to and believed in him. In our long history, men and women have hungered and thirsted for the fullness of life. They have looked to him to find life. Let us look to him who inspires us, by his example, to live life to the fullest.

Chapter 1

JESUS OF NAZARETH: EXEMPLAR OF CONVERSION

My knowledge of affective conversion began by reflecting on my own experience and that of those who came to me for companionship on their spiritual journey. I studied the writings of the fathers and mystics, as well as those of transpersonal psychologists who explore the spiritual dimensions of human experience. These writings were helpful in coming to understand the journey of conversion as it happens to all of us in everyday life. However, through his son Jesus of Nazareth, God remained my principal teacher, bringing together theory with the purifying transitions of my life. The words of scripture became more satisfying and elucidated my perceptions in a deeper way. The Word of God nourished the seed of God within.

My understanding of conversion has deepened and been grounded in coming more and more to know Jesus of Nazareth. He was a man who accepted his incarnation and humanness totally, without question, reserve, or conditions. He grew in age, grace, and wisdom, he learned in the school of experience. He had to grow and learn through the transitional times of his life, just like each of us. He was the complete man. His heritage to us was to come to love in the fullness of its dimensions. It is a love that brings healing and reconciliation, that frees us from living in slavery to the fear of death.

We would rather be like God, as the book of Genesis reminds us. We, who question and want to condition our humanness, differ from him in this. We have an uneasy fixation that we should be other than God made us. Not satisfied with ourselves and chafing under the necessity to learn and grow, we want to be different. Often hidden under this desire is the hope to find a way by which we can avoid the difficulty and vulnerability of living and growing as incarnate men and women.

The author of the Epistle to the Hebrews concentrates our attention on the humanness and experience of Jesus of Nazareth. He points out that Jesus and we share the same humanness. This author stresses that Jesus, who is Lord, did not take flesh from angels but "is truly our blood-brother, a man like ourselves in weakness and temptation, who had to be 'perfected' by the experiences of human life in order that he might become our faithful and compassionate high priest" (Heb 2:17).

Jesus lived through all the transition periods in life from infancy through adolescence to young manhood and beyond. He was "taught in God's school, where the lessons are the experience of temptation and the course a succession of failures and successes" (Margery Kempe et al., p. 80–81). He learned in the school of experience through successes and failures. "Although he was a Son, he learned to obey through suffering" (Heb 5:7–8). To obey means to listen to another and to hear what that one is saying. To obey means that what we hear affects and moves us. It is more like listening and learning with the heart. Jesus' sufferings taught him to listen to God present in his experience. Like all of us, he listened first at the knees of his mother and father. They taught and inspired him. They urged him on when he was afraid and wanted to hold back. They encouraged him when he failed or did not meet others' expectations. They were present to him when he was tried and tested. They celebrated his successes while they corrected him when he was wrong. They taught him to pray and told him about Yahweh and his special relationship to his people. They took him up to Jerusalem to celebrate the great feasts that recalled the wonders that Yahweh had worked to show his continued presence and care. They explained the meaning of his tradition to him so he would keep the word of God in his heart.

As he grew older, he studied the scriptures of his people and learned from them. He was filled with wonder and love for the God who had caused him to be born. He was in awe of the God who entered the lives of his ancestors with promises and covenants. God's enduring efforts and faithfulness to remind people of his love and to carry out his promises inspired Jesus. He became inflamed with the love that God wanted to bring to the world. But he also learned the history of his people's infidelity. He became painfully conscious of a recurring dynamic in the history of his people. They often forgot God's promises. They lost faith and deserted his covenants. He was saddened by their suffering.

Jesus also learned of God's extravagant response to this infidelity in the words of Isaiah. "Because this people approaches me only in words, honors me only with lip-service while its heart is far from me, and my religion, as far as it is concerned, is nothing but human commandment, a lesson memorized, very well, I shall have to go on being prodigal of prodigious prodigies" (Is 29:13–14).

Jesus of Nazareth was a passionate man, son of a passionate God. He yearned for God's promised kingdom. Like many men and women of his day, he waited expectantly for the one whom God would send to liberate his people. Perhaps his reflections on the prophecies made his expectations of the kind of kingdom it might be different from those of his contemporaries. Yet he, too, was filled with a fire and wanted to see his God's kingdom come to reality.

While he continually prayed that the kingdom come, he learned to wait until he discovered what God wanted of him. Then Jesus heard John the Baptist proclaiming a baptism of repentance for the forgiveness of sins. He listened to John preaching that if a tree fails to produce good fruit it will be cut down. When he heard the people asking John, "What must we do?" Jesus was moved by the same question. He asked to be baptized by John in the river Jordan.

Jesus' life was turned upside down. It was a major transition for a carpenter from Nazareth. Perhaps he was not sure what inspired him to be baptized, but he felt it was the right thing to do. He was inspired by John but did not imitate him. He became a teacher and preacher. He stressed the need for repentance, but added that the kingdom of God was close at hand.

Jesus of Nazareth's God was not distant, but very near to him. He was filled with the Spirit of his God. As Jesus began his mission, he was filled with the desire to announce the good news of God's intimate presence in the daily lives of people. He promised God's faithfulness in times of temptation and doubt, and of his care in times of pain and suffering. In Jesus' own life he manifested the love that would drive out the fear that held people in bondage. Jesus wanted them to become spiritually mature so they could appreciate the wonders of God and of life. The gospels tell us how he began this new phase in his life. He announced the first step to spiritual maturity: "The time has come and the kingdom of God is close at hand. Repent and believe the Good News" (Mk 1:15).

His experience and learning intensified during these early years in his interaction with ordinary people, his friends and sinners. In her book *The Passionate God*, Rosemary Haughton shows how Jesus, in interaction with others, gradually came to know himself and his mission (p. 75). Their questions and requests helped him discover his own inner resources that taught him to learn more about himself and his mission. He found that his mission included both foreigners and sinners—all those who desired help and forgiveness. He committed himself to bring good news to the poor, forgiveness to sinners, and freedom to captives.

Jesus of Nazareth's words struck a deep chord in many who listened to him. His sermon on the mount consoled them with its blessings. They desired the abundance of life that he promised. They wondered who this man was who seemed to promise that he would fulfill their longings. He was a man so like themselves. Yet he seemed somehow different. He had a freer spirit, was more filled with a concern for justice and love. He had an interiority that was new to them but attracted them. They found him praying often and he called God, Abba, Father. His passion for the kingdom attracted and excited them. These men and women believed in him. They called him Teacher and Rabbi. They searched their memory of the scriptures and thought that he might be a prophet or the Christ, the one whom God promised. They decided to follow him. Although he came to announce the good news to all, his priority was for the men and women who found faith through him. They were to be the nucleus, the small seed, who would carry on the mission that the whole world needed and so desired to hear.

His learning over the years taught him that these enthusiastic men and women of such goodwill and open and generous hearts were, nevertheless, still blind and deaf. "He could tell what a man had in him" (Jn 2:25). He realized that no one could enter the kingdom that he preached until they were freed from the fear that held them. He knew they could not hear or appreciate the depth of the good news until they could begin to see deeply and to hear clearly. Their divided hearts of stone needed to melt into hearts of flesh as the prophet Ezekiel had prophesied. If they remained faithful, they would be the first to experience the fruit of his mission as it was articulated in Hebrews: "He came to set free all who lived their whole lives in slavery to the fear of death!" (Heb 2:15).

He told them the way to the kingdom was through the conversion to which he was calling them. They would have to be born again into the uncertain ways of the Spirit. To Nicodemus he said:

> I tell you most solemnly, unless a man is born through water and the Spirit, he cannot enter the kingdom of God: what is born of flesh is flesh; what is born of Spirit is spirit. Do not be surprised when I say: You must be born from above. The wind blows wherever it pleases; you hear its sound, but you cannot tell where it comes from or where it is going. That is

how it is with those who are born of the Spirit. . . . I tell you most solemnly, we speak only about what we know and witness to what we have seen (Jn 3:5–8, 11).

Through experience Jesus learned how difficult it was for many people to hear and accept his teaching. He saw how quickly his own disciples forgot what he had said. He did not blame ordinary men and women for their lack of understanding. He realized that deep fears blinded them to the vision of God and deafened them to the voice of God in their hearts. Blind and deaf to God's revelations, they easily forgot his faithfulness; these fears hardened their hearts. Perhaps he learned that his mission would involve something even more radical than preaching and healing.

Another significant turning point in Jesus' life seems to point to that awareness when he took Peter, James, and John up to the mount of Transfiguration. That event "constitutes a breakthrough to a new sphere in the sense of a 'transition' for Jesus himself" (Haughton, p. 79 ff). This earth-shattering experience marks a second transition in Jesus' self-awareness and mission. He begins to be preoccupied with the fact that his teaching and preaching could eventuate in his death. He needed to prepare himself and his friends.

He had begun his teaching by insisting that a new birth must occur, one directly related to a previous death. Passion and death precede rebirth just as passion and death culminate in the resurrection and new life. This new life would give birth to the people of God. As John's gospel approaches the last days of Jesus' earthly life, he tells his friends of another necessity:

I tell you most solemnly, unless a wheat grain falls on the ground and dies, it remains only a single grain; but if it dies, it yields a rich harvest. Anyone who loves his life loses it; anyone who hates his life in this world will keep it for the eternal life (Jn 12:24–25).

Only he knew that if they followed him they would be beginning a life-threatening journey. Their faith would be shaken and stretched to its limits. They would be tempted to doubt and to leave him. Their fears would capture them. Yet he asked them to stand with him in his trials and temptations, in his weakness and tears. He needed their presence and comfort. He had to reassure them continually: "Fear not, I will be with you!"

He knew they would be disappointed in him, that he would not meet their expectations. Though captivated by his personal passion, they feared his total humanness. His weakness and limitations frightened them. The vulnerability of his unrestricted love challenged them. He had learned while he grew in grace and wisdom that his was not a way of arguments and force. It was a way of faithfulness—of a love that would be faithful even unto suffering. When miracles did occur because of his great love, he told the people that it was their faith that had made them whole. His only Testament was not a restoration of Israel's kingdom, but the testimony of his human love that reflected God who is Love. He called them friends. He remembered them. He revealed all to them. They knew how and whom he loved. All he asked of them was to live day by day, step by step, in the here-and-now until the meaning of his good news became clear.

Gradually he learned that they would be scandalized by him. Their fear, turned to terror, would lead them to deny and desert him. He was powerless to help them except with his prayers. He told Peter: "Simon, Simon, Satan, you must know, has got his wish to sift you all like wheat; but I have prayed for you, Simon, that your faith may not fail, and once you have recovered, you in your turn must strengthen your brothers and sisters" (Lk 22:31–32). Only in his passion, death, and resurrection and their own suffering and passion would they be ready to receive Jesus' Spirit. Only with the sending of his own Spirit would the meaning become clear to them. He would have to leave the future in their hands under the inspiration of the Spirit. His life and death would become our gospels.

Jesus' story tells of the personal transformation needed for entry into the kingdom and for mature Christian life. The images show more of a radical break and change than development. They reflect the two most upsetting events in human life: birth and death! The experiences of conversion, of entering the kingdom of God and mature Christian life, are found in the realities of the deaths and rebirths that we find in the fabric and rhythm of human life. These conversion experiences involve fundamental changes in persons: changes from flesh to spirit, from natural to spiritual, from immaturity to maturity, from bondage to freedom, from "living in slavery to the fear of death" (Heb 2:15) to living in the "perfect love which drives out fear" (I Jn 4:18). All these transformations affect our true Self. They occur when we stop clinging to our image of ourselves that we have constructed so that our "hidden self" can grow strong and Jesus of Nazareth can live in our hearts through faith. Then we can be guided by the Spirit.

Chapter 2

THE KINGDOM OF GOD IS WITHIN

Jesus of Nazareth began his public life proclaiming good news from God. "The time has come," he said, "the kingdom of God is close at hand" (Mk 1:15). Jesus expected that the kingdom he was passionate for was very near. According to the evangelists he said: "I tell you truly, there are some standing here who will not taste death before they see the kingdom of God" (Lk 9:27). He used many parables to tell what the kingdom of God was like. Then he explained the parables to his followers. Teaching about the "Kingdom of God" was central to his mission.

His teaching had a great impact on the Jewish people who expected that the kingdom begun by King David was to be restored. Jesus' words heightened that hope and their expectations. That he might be the "king of the Jews" stirred up fear in the authorities in Jerusalem, who promoted his death. After his death and resurrection, the apostles expected Jesus to come again shortly to establish his kingdom. His imminent return was a central belief among the early Christians.

When the apostles had pressed Jesus to tell them when the kingdom would come, he told them he did not know. While the apostles struggled to understand what Jesus may have meant by saying that the kingdom of God was at hand, they began to remember that he had told them that "the Kingdom of God is already among you," within you (Lk 17:21). They soon realized that Jesus was speaking primarily of an interior kingdom of truth and love, where truth is not static or carved on stone. It is alive, continually revealing, written in the hearts of men and women. Love was to be shown in deed as well as in word.

With his background in the Hebrew scriptures, Saint Paul remembered passages from Deuteronomy 30 where the people were told that "the Word of God is very near to you, it is in your mouth and in your heart for your observance" (Dt 30:12–14). Saint Paul recognized that the same admonition applied to Jesus of Nazareth. "Do not tell yourself you have to bring Christ down [from heaven] or that you have to bring Christ back from the dead. The Word, that is the faith we proclaim is very near to you, it is on your lips and in your heart" (Rom 10:6–8).

In addition to telling us where we must look and what we must listen to, Saint Paul is more explicit about how we find faith in Jesus. We discover him in what he calls our "hidden self." In other places he calls it our "True Self." There we can experience Jesus living within us. In this dynamic relationship we will find the many riches of the kingdom that Jesus taught. Paul prays:

> May he [God] give you the power through his Spirit for your hidden self to grow strong, so that Christ may live in your hearts through faith, and then, planted in love and built on love, you will with all the saints have strength to grasp the breadth and the length, the height and the depth; until, knowing the

love of Christ you are filled with the utter
fullness of God (Eph 3:16–19).

Saint Paul tells us that it is *within ourselves* where we
find the riches of God. His prayer points out the path to the
development of spiritual maturity. He stresses the steps in
the process to find the Word of God who is very close to us.
We start by becoming strong in knowing our hidden self.
Once we begin to know ourselves, Christ can begin to live
in our hearts. Finally, by continuing to know ourselves and
Christ's living presence in our hearts, we discover the
boundless riches of God. We must go through a series of
changes and growth so we can be born again. It brings us to
the place where we experientially find God in Jesus of
Nazareth and in ourselves. When our hidden self grows
strong, we begin to truly know ourselves. In that
knowledge we also know God in Jesus of Nazareth, as Saint
Augustine tells us: "Let me know myself, Lord, so I may
know you."

Despite this exhortation of Saint Paul and his promise
of the riches, we recognize the feat that grips us when we
are asked to go inside. We fear what we do not know and
may not be able to control. We are fearful of our unknown,
hidden self. Jung calls it our "undiscovered self." When we
are asked to examine what is in our hearts and on our lips,
some of our dreams and unsolicited impulses can leave us
afraid of what we might find there. Perhaps behind the
façade of our outer personality hides someone who is very
different from the self we know. If others knew of the
thoughts, inclinations, and feelings that can inhabit our
minds, our fear might turn into panic. This fear can become
a many-headed monster, bordering on terror and dread. We
fear the journey and the effort it might take.

We should not minimize the difficulty involved in meeting our hidden self. Nor should we judge this encounter to be beyond our strength. It is God who calls us at the edges of ourselves, at our arid places. He invites us to enter the unknown and unlived parts of ourselves. These are the places where we are dead and not yet alive, the uncultivated parts of ourselves that need to be cleared and made fertile. When we enter them, they can spring into life.

We are urged to explore and to know our desert, the untamed wilderness within that frightens and haunts us. We condemn and banish those parts of ourselves that we judge unclean and unacceptable. We try to disown them and we drive them into our hidden self. In the book of Micah we find the author naming these parts "Unloved" and "No People of Mine." We hide behind our persona, our false self, hoping that it will make us invisible and invulnerable to others, and to God. Unfortunately we become blind to ourselves too. When we drop our familiar mask, our fear can turn to terror. What we have tried to hide and bury is uncovered. By entering these places of our hidden self, we become vulnerable so that God can break through in his amazing ways to bring us forgiveness, healing, and reconciliation.

People in every age have written about the difficulty we experience when we are forced to confront ourselves, to find what is in our hearts. Some people describe the experience of entering the hidden self as being caught in a wild whirlpool that drags us down to its center. Helplessly we descend and encounter the monsters of the deep. We are in darkness. We fear we will drown. We do not like the vulnerability of the pilgrim that we must become when we leave familiar territory to enter our desert.

The pilgrim's way, reflected in the book of Sirach, reminds us of just how fearful the journey is.

> ... for though she [Wisdom] takes him at first through winding ways, bringing fear and faintness on him, plaguing him with her discipline until she can trust him, and testing him with her ordeals, in the end she will lead him back to the straight road, and reveal her secrets to him (Sir 4:17–18).

Henri Nouwen describes the challenge and the difficulty we can experience when we enter our hidden self.

> The inward man is faced with a new and often dramatic task. He must come to terms with the inner tremendum. Just as the God outside could be experienced not only as a loving father but also as a horrible demon, the God within can be not only a source of new creative life but also the cause of chaotic confusion (p. 37).

Psychologist Carl Jung writes about the great reluctance people experience when invited to explore their unknown, hidden self. He tells about the extremes people will go to so they can avoid this confrontation. This is especially true of middle-aged people who have lived long enough to know failures as well as successes. Edwin Aldrin, the second man to walk on the moon, had a mental breakdown after he came back to earth. He had been forced to face himself and his life. He had to uncover his own as well as his family's secrets. After his recovery, he called this confrontation with himself the last frontier, the most difficult.

Evelyn Underhill, a noted writer on spirituality, explored the world of religious experience and mysticism. She used Teresa of Avila's imagery of the "Interior Castle" as a model for the hidden self and the process of growth in spiritual development. She calls her exposition *The House of the Soul*. Like Teresa, who insists that we only approach our hidden self with Jesus of Nazareth, she emphasizes the humanity, the humanness of Jesus. It is the man, Jesus, who, like us in all things, inspires us. She writes:

> The strength of this house [of the soul] consisted in that intimate welding of the divine and the human, which she [Teresa of Avila] found in its perfection in the humanity of Christ. There, in the common stuff of human life which He blessed with His presence, the saints have ever seen the homely foundation of holiness (p. 6).

She tells us that we must go into every room of our house from the basement to the attic. Usually, we like to show others and even ourselves only our parlor where we keep everything shined and polished. But she tells us we must explore and clean all the rooms, including the basement, where Saint Teresa says we are likely to find damp unpleasant corners and reptiles and other horrors lurking (p. 13).

Underhill claims that Teresa of Avila says "the best way [to approach the Interior Castle] is to strive to enter first by the room where humility is practiced, which is far better than at once rushing off to the others" (p. 13). Rooted in our own humanness, but without judging ourselves, we will find the humility necessary to begin. Underhill reminds us that:

A full and wholesome spiritual life can never consist in living upstairs, and forgetting to consider the ground floor. . . . Nor does it consist in the constant, exasperated investigation of the shortcomings of the basement. . . . Since we are two-story creatures, called to a natural and supernatural status, both sense and spirit must be rightly maintained (p. 6).

Henri Nouwen tells us what we must do when we enter the confusing world of our hidden self.

The first and most basic task . . . is to clarify the immense confusion that can arise when people enter this new internal world . . . to enter our selves first of all into the center of our existence and become familiar with the complexities of our inner lives. As soon as we feel at home in our own house, discover the dark corners as well as the light spots, the closed doors as well as the drafty rooms, our confusion will evaporate, our anxiety will diminish, and we will become capable of creative work (pp. 37–38).

Recognizing the difficulties and dangers of exploring this inner world alone, we might find a spiritual guide helpful, if not necessary. Henri Nouwen advises that people who would enter the ministry of spiritual companionship, whether it be as pastoral ministers, retreat givers, or spiritual directors, need to know the stirrings of their own interior world. He knew that we do not allow other people to go where we ourselves have not gone or are fearful to go.

Perhaps he recalled Jesus' admonition to the Pharisees in the gospel of Matthew. "Alas for you scribes and Pharisees, you hypocrites! You who shut up the kingdom of heaven in men's faces, neither going in yourselves nor allowing others to go in who want to" (Mt 23:13). He emphasizes what is needed for us who enter the interior world of the hidden self and for people who would become companions to others.

> The [person] who can articulate the movements of his inner life, who can give names to his varied experiences, need no longer be a victim of himself, but is able . . . to create space for Him whose heart is greater than his, whose eyes see more than his, and whose hands can heal more that his. This articulation is the basis for spiritual leadership of the future (Nouwen, p. 38).

We must go within, pay attention to, and take seriously what we discover in our hidden self. There are affective feelings and emotions with their movements and changes. We will find moods, memories, dreams, symbols, fantasies, and deep inspirations. We must accept what we find without judgment. There will be places of freedom and of constraint, of light and darkness. Some we welcome; many are frightening; others we want to deny. We must not take these discoveries at face value nor reject them. It is important to stay with them until they can mature and reveal themselves to us. Remember that everything we find is part of our reality and must be freed into life. If God does not reject us, why should we reject ourselves?

Chapter 3

SHATTERED HOPES

As we begin our mid-life passage we seem to find our way blocked. The pattern and rhythm of our lives change. What we had hoped and worked for now seems empty and worthless. The beliefs on which we constructed our lives, which brought us meaning and purpose, now lay at our feet like the counterfeit ranting of a bogus teacher. Our trust level sinks to zero. The bottom drops out, our lives seem built on shifting sands. We are disillusioned and desperate. We suffer from the disappointment and confusion that accompanies our shattered dreams. We want to believe we are mistaken. We want deny the failure of our hopes, but we recognize that would be a false hope.

Perhaps our disillusionment is like that of the very early Christians who had great hopes and expectations. After the resurrection, the apostles enthusiastically had begun to preach the good news that Jesus from Nazareth is Lord, the one whom God had promised. They taught that the kingdom of God that he preached would come soon for those who believed. They stressed his promise that the kingdom he proclaimed was at hand. The first Christians had high expectations of life after their baptism by the apostles. They looked forward to a new kingdom like the one established by King David and Solomon. They showed the fervor of new converts. The Acts of the Apostles tells us about the hopes and idealism of these early Christians. "They remained faithful to the teaching of the apostles, to the brotherhood, to the breaking of bread, and to the prayers. . . . The faithful all lived together and owned everything in common; they sold their goods and possessions and shared out of the proceeds among themselves according to what each one needed" (Acts 2:41–45).

The apostles had been convinced that Jesus' coming again was imminent and prepared their fledgling community for the new kingdom. After many years of weary waiting, it became clear that Jesus was not coming in their lifetime. When his expected return did not materialize, the apostles came to realize that their understanding of the kingdom must have been wrong. Then they remembered that Jesus had told them that no one, not even he, knew the time when the kingdom would arrive. It became clear to them that their teaching about the imminence of the kingdom was incorrect. The kingdom was not going to come soon. They had to admit to their early converts that they had been mistaken in their belief. The goal of Jesus' life did not center on the restoration of former kingdoms—he had another purpose.

The faith of the early Christians was shattered. They were disillusioned. Whom could they believe? Could they trust both Jesus of Nazareth and the teaching of the apostles? It was the "mid-life crisis" for these early Christians. From a new perspective of disappointment and confusion they asked: Who is this Son of God who was Jesus of Nazareth? If he is not going to establish his kingdom, who is he and why did he come? What does he ask of us?

The apostles' thoughts returned to the Jesus they knew when he was among them. Their experience of the years spent walking with Jesus and listening to him taught them a new understanding of his mission. He had not come to fulfill an unnatural desire of ours to wipe our slate clean and have a new beginning. He had not come to restore an innocence that only the sinless have. He had not come to free us from all of the infirmities that come with being human. Then they began to realize that Jesus of Nazareth's life was meant to inspire us to live our own unique lives as truthfully and faithfully as he lived his. He had come to show us how to live in love. Even though the fullness of the kingdom would come later, it was present already among those who believed in and were inspired by Jesus.

It was in this milieu of broken promises and dashed expectations that the Epistle to the Hebrews was composed. The author concentrates our attention on the humanness and experience of Jesus of Nazareth. He stresses that Jesus, who is Lord, "is truly our blood-brother, a man like ourselves in weakness and temptation, who had to be 'perfected' by the experiences of human life in order that he might become our faithful and compassionate high priest" (Barnabas Ahern, p. 13).

The author of Hebrews simply insists that Jesus' incarnate life was the same as ours, and tells us why:

> Since all children share the same blood and flesh, he too shared equally in it, so that by his death he could take away all the power of the devil, who had power over death, and *set free all those who had been held in slavery all their*

> *lives by the fear of death.* . . . It was essential that he should in this way become completely like his brothers so that he could be a compassionate and trustworthy high priest of God's religion, able to atone for sins. Because he has himself been through temptation he is able to help others who are tempted (Heb 2:14–18, emphasis mine).

Jesus came to free us from living in fear and its slavery that incites us to sin. The author continues to point out that Jesus is not only like us in birth, but also in humanness. He had to learn in the school of human experience. He was weak and limited, had feelings and temptations.

> It is not as if we had a high priest who was incapable of feeling our weaknesses with us; but we have one who has been tempted in every way we are, though he is without sin (Heb 4:15).

> He can sympathize with those who are ignorant or uncertain because he too lives in the limitations of weakness. That is why he has to make sin offerings for himself as well as for the people (Heb 5:1–3).

> During his life on earth, he offered up prayer and entreaty, aloud and silent tears, to the one who had the power to save him out of death, and he submitted so humbly that his prayer was heard. Although he was son, he learned to obey through suffering (Heb 5:7–8).

When the author of Hebrews speaks of the "perfecting" of Jesus, he implies that Jesus had to live through all the transition times in life that can be so upsetting. He had to learn how to come to know himself, to care for others, to live more integrally, and to love abundantly. No one teaches us how to navigate these fundamental human challenges. Others serve as models. They inspire us. They urge us on when we want to quit. They can encourage us when we falter and fail. But all of us have to learn on our own through our life experiences how to come to human, spiritual maturity. We will be tested and tried. The letter to the Hebrews wisely reminds us that temptation is the necessary road we must travel to come to full humanness and to become compassionate and trustworthy persons. We will succeed and fail. All of these trying times help us to grow. They teach us true compassion born of the passion of suffering and the passion of love. They all lead to the fullness of being human.

Kirkegaard claims that no one can teach us how to satisfy these fundamental human needs. We all must learn them on our own. I find an example of this in an infant learning to walk. Walking is within him; no one "teaches" him or her this skill. We may encourage, cajole, praise, or scold, but a child learns to walk on its own. A cover on a *Parade* magazine some years ago displayed in a series of pictures the feelings on a little girl's face when she was finally learning to walk. There was such determination, discouragement, and elation when she finally stood on her own.

The writers of the scriptures tell us of Jesus learning in the school of experience. The fathers and mystics realized more deeply and keenly that every Christian has to learn as Jesus learned in the school of experience. This learning can be a long and arduous process. We make mistakes. We have successes and failures. We may try over and over again. We give up for a while before trying again, trying from a different angle. We often have to wait a long time before learning occurs. Change is a hallmark of this life process. Cardinal Newman wrote: "In a higher world it is otherwise, but here below to live is to change, and to be perfect is to have changed often." Change both excites and challenges us. It is also what we most resist out of fear.

The letter to the Hebrews gives us the reasons why Jesus needed to come as a man like us. He came to inspire us to accept the gift of incarnation more fully. He came so that we could trust him and accept his merciful forgiveness. He came to become a friend.

How do we relate to this man who through weakness and limitation, temptation and suffering became our compassionate high priest? How do we ask the question, "Who is Jesus of Nazareth"? We are accustomed to calling him Christ using the words of the apostles. We call him Lord, which is how we learned to proclaim him after his death. But each of us must first ask, "Who is Jesus of Nazareth for me"?

We find our response to that question by asking ourselves how we accept our own humanity, our humanness. How do we accept ourselves? The scriptures tell us that Jesus accepted his humanness fully and totally without conditions or limitations. He entered into every essential human experience. His life challenges us to ask how we have accepted this gift of being human.

At first we may be surprised that we find this question addressed to us. On reflection we may discover that we have reservations about our humanness. How often we would like to be different: a little taller, smarter, older, younger. Our envies reveal these reservations to us. We put limits and conditions on the humanness we accept. We may disown our body as well as our spirit, denying those parts of ourselves that we are ashamed of, disapprove of, or fear. We hide what we judge unclean or unworthy and try to banish those aspects from our lives. We may deny our anger or our sexuality. We live in slavery to our fear. We excuse our failures, mistakes, and sins. We try to cover them over, explain them away, justify our actions. All these aspects of ourselves are not acceptable to that someone in us who desires to be god-like. How many of our mental illnesses, not physically caused, stem from the fact that we refuse and deny our humanness? Psychosomatic illnesses arise out of distortions in accepting our humanness. The most unfortunate of all even give up on life altogether.

We may have come to believe that because Jesus of Nazareth is the Son of God, he is much more than we are. Such belief is contrary to the claims in the letter to the Hebrews and is a false assumption. We think his special gifts set him apart from us. We judge that he is unapproachable, not another man like us, a brother. By doing this, we cleverly and subtly twist the truth. We make ourselves the norm and a criterion of who a human really is. That assumption distorts the whole revelation and meaning of the Incarnation. The real question is how much *less* than human have we become than he who is the fullness of being human. He was limited, weak, and tempted. He had to learn through experience, had to go through stages of growth and change so he could live and speak his word. He accepted change and limitations. He suffered and died. Instead of striving to be god-like, we must strive to be like Jesus of Nazareth. We must accept the challenges of life rather then avoiding them.

The author of Hebrews dispels the error that grows out of this false assumption that still infects men and women who blame the trials of life and their sins on their humanness. They desire to be like angels, thinking they would be freed from these burdens. Writing of Jesus' birth the author insists that "it was not the angels he took to himself; he took to himself descent from Abraham. . . . We do see in Jesus one who was for a short while made lower than the angels and is now crowned with glory and splendor because he submitted to death; by God's grace he had to experience death for all mankind" (Heb 2:9).

The fact that the Son of God is both Jesus of Nazareth, completely human, and Jesus the Lord, completely God, has given rise to strong disagreements in every age and conflicts for individuals. It has been the battleground of much controversy and has spawned heresies. This dilemma between emphasizing one aspect of either the Lord the Christ or Jesus of Nazareth continues and challenges every individual. There is a tendency in all of us to discount or ignore the full implications that Jesus the Lord, the Christ, was really human like us. Like early Christians we expect the Lord our God to be above us, to be able to do anything, to be a miracle worker. It is easy to forget that he was human, limited, tempted, and weak like we are. Many of us seem to go back and forth between emphasizing either the Lord our God or Jesus from Nazareth until we come to "experience" that Jesus of Nazareth *is* Lord. It is not a matter of choosing between one or the other, Jesus is both human *and* Lord. It is not a matter of concepts, but of lived experience.

In our own time those at Vatican Council II needed to reiterate this truth for themselves and for us. The council's statement points to the complete humanness of Jesus, but it lacks the vitality and concreteness we find in the letter to the Hebrews. The decree *Gaudium et Spes* proclaims:

> Jesus himself was the perfect man. He worked with human hands, He thought with a human mind, acted by human choice, and loved with a human heart (pp. 220–221).

We find how difficult it is to realize the full implications of our belief that Jesus of Nazareth was truly man and truly God. The second-century Gnostic heresy denied the teaching in Hebrews. It claimed that human beings are intrinsically base and perverse with the conclusion that Jesus could not be truly a man. It taught that Jesus only appeared to be a human but was actually a divine "messenger."

Saint Irenaeus, a follower of Polycarp, fought the false claims of the Gnostics. He taught that Jesus—and every person—lives through the cycles and stages of salvation history. He found the roots of this in Saint Paul who prayed that our hidden self grow strong so that we gradually come to God. Irenaeus writes of Jesus: "When he became Incarnate and was made man, he recapitulated in himself the long history of man, summing up and giving us salvation in order that we might receive again in Christ Jesus what we had lost in Adam, i.e., the image and likeness of God" (*Advesus hereses*, 3, 18, 7).

Jean Danielou comments very simply on what Irenaeus says about the imperfection of God's creation, and why people sin. Danielou says:

> if man has been created in a state of imperfection, it is not due to God's inability to create him perfect, nor to some catastrophe

in a previous world, owing to some earlier sin: it is simply the very essence of created things to have a beginning, a development, and a fulfillment (Jean Danielou, S.J., pp. 33–34).

Danielou quotes Irenaeus himself where he stresses the necessity of stages of growth.

God could have given perfection to man from the start; but this would have been too much for one but newly created. . . . According to the divine plan man has been created in the image and likeness of God the uncreated, the Father approving and commanding [in his Love], the Son performing and creating [in his Love], the Spirit giving nourishment and growth [in his Love], and *man gradually advancing and coming to perfection.* It was needful that man should first be brought into being, and being made should grow, and having grown should come to manhood, and after manhood should be multiplied and being multiplied should grow in strength, and after such growth should be glorified and being glorified should see his own Lord. Those then are every way unreasonable who, not waiting for the time of growth, charge God with the infirmity of their own nature. They neither know God nor themselves, insatiable and ungrateful. They are even unwilling to be what they are made, men capable of passions. But overstepping the law of mankind, already, even before they are

made, men want to be like unto God their
Maker (IV, 38; 1107 BC) (pp. 35–36, emphasis
mine).

We often display that unnatural desire to be like God
which leads to sin. Irenaeus claims that we sin when we do
not mature according to our age. We try to skip over or slow
down stages of growth. We seem to have great trouble with
the laws of natural growth. When we are young, we want to
hurry it along. How many boys and girls skip part of the
play and fun of childhood so they can become little men or
little women? How often in early adulthood do we aspire to
gain a status that is beyond our age or experience? We want
to be wise before our time. As we get older we would like to
slow the process down. We would rather remain at forty
and holding. We want to be in control of our lives, thinking
that we are like God. But we are not godly.

To blame our bodily existence for our faults and sins
seems to confront all of us from time to time. How often do
we hear "I am only human"? Irenaeus tells us that this
stems from our wanting to be like God. We want to be in
control. We forget the words used by God in the Hebrew
Testament and quoted by the author of Hebrews referring
to Jesus: "This is what he said on coming into the world:
'You who wanted no sacrifice or oblation, prepared a body
for me. You took no pleasure in holocausts or sacrifices for
sin; then I said, just as I was commanded in the scroll of the
book, God, here I am! I am coming to do your will'"(Heb
10:5–7).

As we reflect on our own and Jesus' humanity, it may
be helpful to hear how Teilhard de Chardin worded his
response to the question about who Jesus the Man was.
Toward the end of his life he came to appreciate God's love

for men and the world. He wrote: "To the full extent of my powers, *because I am a priest*, I would be more widely human in my sympathies than any of the world's servants" (T. de Chardin, p. 128).

Chapter 4

DYNAMICS OF CONVERSION: DENIAL AND ANGER

Our shattered hopes and spoiled dreams leave us in hopeless and helpless confusion. We are powerless to halt this cancer of meaning and purpose. With some fear, we may enter our kingdom within or we may continue on the fruitless search for meaning outside ourselves. Later, on reflection, we recognize that our spirit, hungering and thirsting for something more, had sensed the promise of bread and new life. It will not rest until it breaks through our constraints that hold it captive. We may try to rationalize our experience until our minds grow weary with effort, but the effort yields no results. Feeling betrayed and angry, we begin to grumble and complain that life is not what we expected it to be. We must seek personal meaning and relief from our dis-ease of spirit that comes from inside us. We must pay attention to the bewildering mixture of feelings and emotions that emerge.

Our feelings and emotions are there to greet us when we enter our kingdom within. They are like the guardians of our inner world. Our feelings are our first and most primitive way of knowing. Long before our minds develop their more sophisticated ways, our feelings and emotions tell us about ourselves and others. They move and affect us. They help us to know what is on our lips and in our hearts. They reveal the condition and health of the life of our spirit.

I found it helpful to read Dr. Elisabeth Kübler-Ross' descriptions of the feelings and emotions of patients with terminal illnesses whom she studied. She observed five stages that individuals ordinarily go through during the course of a final illness. In her book *On Death and Dying,* she named them denial, anger, bargaining, depression, and, finally, acceptance. These stages are not step-by-step phases even though they show a progression. The five dynamics are present all the time, while we become aware of the various ones at different times. As each dynamic grows in intensity, it rises to the surface of our awareness. It is something like the bubbling of a pot of soup when different ingredients rise in turn to the top again and again. It is like the development of a fetus where different parts develop unevenly until it becomes a viable infant. Our mid-life passages and conversions share these same patterns with the terminally ill.

Reading Kübler-Ross's descriptions, we find that these spontaneous reactions are similar to what we go through during those wrenching times of change in our lives. Upon reflection they are very familiar and close to us. They are part of life, the dying and rising that we find everyday. These dynamics are woven into the fabric of life from our earliest days. We discover them when we reach our limits and need to enter new stages of life: in learning to walk and to talk, in tolerating a new sibling, in daily interactions with others, in new situations.

In conversion times, we do not climb higher and higher on the road to God. God forces us to search ourselves and the limits and boundaries that we have imposed on ourselves. He calls for the breakthrough that our conversion announces when our feelings and emotions intensify. Though some traumatic event may have triggered the beginning, we realize gradually that our need for change stems from some inner need. In these desert places, we become aware of our idols and idealizations; we long for authenticity. We become vulnerable in a new way with the helplessness of a lost child crying for its mother or of someone longing for a lover.

When the ease of our life's flow is blocked and stopped, we are shocked out of our familiar world. Our security, safety, control, and identity are threatened. We reach our limits and are catapulted into insecurity. Our defenses seem to crumble. Our "who I am" is questioned and attacked. The wildness around us begins to threaten.

Everything goes stale. What once was filled with flavor for us is now empty. Life becomes tasteless. The salt that once brought savor to life now only grinds us irritatingly. Where we once went with enthusiasm, we now have to drag ourselves through rituals that have become meaningless.

We feel a sense of alienation, of being a stranger who is no longer at home in a familiar place. Everything and everyone is the same, yet somehow different. We feel like a foreigner in what had seemed our native land. We feel we have been uprooted. Our familiar world loses its solidity, its obviousness, its security. We seem to have lost our bearings and directions. We find that the beginning of Dante's *Divine Comedy* describes our experience. "Midway upon the journey of life, I found that I was in a dusky wood, for the right path, whence I had strayed, was lost."

At first we may ignore what seems to be happening to us. We think that perhaps it will go away. At the same time, we become more aware of the frayed edges of our lives—not enough attention to our spouse or family, not enough dedication at work, not enough faithfulness to God. We may become compulsively busy. We feel from past experience that "if something is wrong, I must be responsible for it." We tend to make promises only to break them over and over again.

When we become frightened, we tend to rely on our heads. We try to cut off our affective experience as if it were the cause of the problem. Many literally "choke down" their affections. We become extremely heady or wordy. When we squeeze our emotions our head gets puffed up and dictatorial. Our inner judge or counselor sets up such a clamor with his many opinions that we fear we may go crazy. We cannot listen to our hearts.

When nothing seems to stop the invading dis-ease, a deep aloneness settles over us, a disturbing loneliness in which we experience a growing distance from others. We feel we are traveling a different road, rarely traveled. Like a terminally ill patient, we may judge that this is a final journey. But we do not know where the journey is leading or when or even whether we will arrive. This aloneness is different from the loneliness we may have experienced before, and it comes from another, deeper place within us. Meaning fades from our lives. A gray pall of meaninglessness begins to descend.

Perhaps what gives this condition its unique, personal texture is that nagging and gnawing questions begin to arise from within. "What is my life about?" "Where am I going?" "Does anything really matter?" "What does it all mean?" "Who am I?" We have learned the answers to these questions since we heard them as children from our parents. As adults, we have confirmed them many times over the years. We have lived them. But the questions persist and gnaw at us. Familiar answers no longer satisfy. They mock us. It is as though these questions arise from someone inside who we do not know. They are being asked of us in an intensely personal way. They are no longer theoretical questions, but questions about our own lives. They are fundamental, vital questions arising from our hidden selves. We are face to face with the antinomies of life: of life and death, of love and care, of truth and lies. The refrain from the song "The Rose" that "it seems that love is only for the lucky and the strong" becomes our lament. We ask whether there can be life in this dying.

Our denial grows as this dis-ease of the spirit continues. We refuse to believe what is occurring. Denial can be our refusal to be touched and moved by the radical change taking place in our lives. We wrap ourselves in the cloak of our willpower so nothing can touch us. We take the defiant stance of the "stoic."

> It may thus come about that by accepting an inevitable destiny which I refuse with all my strength to anticipate, I will find a way of inward consolidation, of proving my reality to myself, and at the same time I shall rise infinitely above this *fatum* to which I have never allowed myself to shut my eyes (Gabriel Marcel, p. 38).

Marcel says the willful stoic "affords us the highest expression, the greatest degree of sublimation of the 'I myself.' Herein without any doubt lies the power and greatness of stoicism, but at the same time it must be recognized that the stoic is always imprisoned within himself. He strengthens himself, but he does not radiate" (p. 38).

Many others call upon the "optimist." With a fixed smile the optimist has a firm conviction, or just a vague feeling, that things tend to "turn out for the best." He does not rely on an experience that comes from the most intimate and living part of himself or his experience. He keeps things at a sufficient distance and so he is not affected. The optimist lives off the coin of another. The optimist has all kinds of quick clichés to address every situation. We recognize the optimist by Marcel's description, "The optimist is essentially a maker of speeches" (p. 34).

We are ambivalent at this time about all that is happening in us. We are not sure we can trust ourselves and others. Sometimes we can talk about it. Other times we feel a need to remain silent. Some denial can be good and necessary, for it serves as a buffer to allow us to collect ourselves, to mobilize ourselves with less radical defenses so that we can cope with what is occurring. We are getting ready for the journey and we must prepare. Some aloneness and distance is not escape, but a necessary admission that something is going on, that a death is occurring. You cannot put your hands on death, but you can gradually learn to fear it less and to live with it day by day. There was a television program some years ago about a young athlete who was stricken by a deadly disease. In the film he spent many hours walking alone along a beach. He was healing his spirit.

An added burden to individuals suffering from this sickness of spirit may come from the people around them. Denial can increase in us when those close to us are in denial, when they cannot face or appreciate our present condition. Counselors or clergymen who have not come face to face with the suffering of that pain and death of conversion in their own lives can frustrate us. They seem to have such quick and sure answers to our suffering. They may give us a stoic's advice to face what is happening within us like an adult. Or, like an optimist, they may talk about God's love, providence, heaven, suffering, but at an abstract distance that avoids the present nitty-gritty of our real suffering. Their patronizing professionalism both angers and depresses us.

When this cancer of "spirit and meaning" continues to spread and deepen, the arms of our mind are bound and held fast. We are powerless. We can do nothing. No matter how stupid and simple the vital questions may seem, we cannot find the answers. We grumble.

These questions cause a tremendous dissonance within us. We experience the clash of our values, ideals, and goals with the reality of our personal lives. Now the trumpet of the need for change increases the clamor. Yet we do not know what we want or need. Our compulsiveness seems to switch into high gear, to new energy levels. We become judgmental and demanding. We become experts at seeing the faults in others while failing to recognize our own.

As these vital questions push deeper into our spirit, they must be answered. But we are unable to respond to or control them. All our old ways and means of dealing with problems come to naught. We cannot find the inner resources. This is often disconcerting because we may have reached great heights in developing our powers and our personal capacity. We are brought to the point of vulnerability and crisis, of breakthrough or breakdown.

The writer Leo Tolstoy describes his experience of being assaulted by these vital questions in the prime of his life when he was acknowledged as a great writer. He thought his life had stopped. Simple questions became vitally important to him but unanswerable in his accustomed way. What he had based his life on seemed to have collapsed and shattered around him. He feared he was becoming mentally ill.

The author James Baldwin illustrates the urgency of these vital questions. He claims they have a haunting quality. He also points out that if we allow them to yeast and to open us they may lead to understanding and compassion. Because of the color of his skin, he had fled to Europe where he felt there would be less discrimination. When, after an agonizing debate within himself, he returned from his self-imposed exile, he published a work that described the anguish and anxiety that these questions had caused him. Writing about his time in Europe he says:

> But I still believe the unexamined life is not worth living; and I know that self-delusion, in the service of no matter what small or lofty cause, is a price no writer can afford. . . . But the question which confronted me, nibbled at me, in my Corsican exile was: Am I afraid of returning to America? Or am I afraid of journeying any further with myself? Once this question had presented itself it would not be appeased, it had to be answered. . . . The questions which one asks oneself begin, at last, to illuminate the world, and become one's key to the experience of others. One can only face in others what one can face in oneself. On this confrontation depends the measure of our wisdom and compassion (Introduction).

Our anger signals and increases our powerlessness. Anger is the flip side of powerlessness and a multi-faceted experience. We use it in an attempt to fight for control and to move against the forces invading us. We are looking for values to stand on or to stand for. In the face of "powerlessness," which means I cannot *do* what I want, anger is the defiant stance that I *can*. Most people seem to think of anger as an explosive tantrum or outburst that will destroy others and oneself. But anger has many faces and voices: rage, resentment, jealousy, envy, stubbornness, self-pity which is turned into anger, coldness, sarcasm, silence, irony, criticism, biting back, killing another with kindness, deep vindictiveness.

Anger is often non-specific, "free-floating." We find ourselves, often to our amazement, to be an "angry" person. We find an aggressiveness creeping in that is foreign to us. It makes us want to hit and pound. We displace it onto slamming doors, or road rage. We project it onto those who appear weaker or more vulnerable, those who cannot or will not fight back. We may introject anger, becoming angry with ourselves because the anger has shown us to be vulnerable and out of control. It can turn into a vicious circle.

We should not be shocked by the disproportionate anger we experience in a particular situation. It can be traced to the pools of anger within us, the angers we tried to sit on in the past. The present situation touches all the unexpressed, primitive, and unresolved angers in our life. We discover that the angry infant, adolescent, young man or woman are still alive and active. All the anger from situations in the past is still alive and being held in our body.

Our anger can also be directed toward God, who we thought was the source of all good and providence. Such anger is a reaction to the consequences of our original, fundamental sin, to rejection, to being driven out of Paradise. We may be angry that God did not consult us about being born. We were not included in decisions about our parents, sex, nationality. Who is this God who is behind this dying and who permits such injustice? Silvano Arieti writes that "All will has its source in the capacity to say 'No.' The 'No' is a protest against a world we never made, and it is also an assertion of one's self" (quoted in Rollo May, *Love and Will*, p. 284).

This anger is also directed toward those who use God as a shield or a weapon, finding a target in the church, or individuals who use their authority to make themselves "gods." It grows toward those people whom we have made "gods" in our own lives by giving them too much authority. Angry people have great expertise at *echolalia*, speaking others' truths without exploring their own or others' reality.

If others understand these feelings of powerlessness and anger, it is easier for us to express and to be present to the anger. If others have faced their own fears and their aggressive and destructive tendencies, they can stand with us. They can allow others to be with their anger and to find "frustrated love." It is the stance of the little boy or girl who says, "You don't love me and I am angry!" There is no logic in love or anger!

Chapter 5

DYNAMICS OF CONVERSION: ANXIETY AND GRIEVING

Persistent questions about life and identity that arise from within at mid-life demand to be answered. They intensify into the cruel struggle that Shakespeare tells us troubled Hamlet: to be or not to be, that is the question. Denial and anger exhaust us. Now meaninglessness touches and enshrouds us. The struggle itself seems like a devilish charade. Thomas Merton succinctly observes,

> Questions that have answers seem, at such a time, to be a cruel mockery of the helpless mind. Existence itself becomes an absurd question, and to find the answer to such a question is to be irrevocably lost (pp. 3–4).

With the meaning and purpose of our lives threatened, we sense we are on the brink of existence. Something beyond our control threatens to overwhelm us. An unknown malevolent force seems to be stalking us. We may experience a fear of an unexpected and violent death akin to the tragedy of September 11, 2001. This can easily turn into a fear of life as a whole. Anxiety besieges us. Like Chicken

Little we can think that "the sky is falling." It seems to spread a pervasive threat and gloom over us like the dark cloud following Joe Btfsplk in Al Capp's comic strip "Li'l Abner."

Anxiety springs up from our depths, from the same place that the question about our identity arises. It signals a threat from within, not from without. It is rooted in our being as a person, writes Rollo May, a psychotherapist, who finds its source in the fact that our existence is given to us without our consent. And it may be taken away equally abruptly. The resulting deep fear leaves us vulnerable. He calls this "existential anxiety" and claims that

> It is always a threat to the foundation, the center, of my existence. Basic anxiety is the experience of the threat of imminent non-being. . . . Anxiety is the subjective state of the individual's becoming aware that his existence can become destroyed, that he can lose himself and his world, that he can become "nothing." It strikes the core of self-esteem and self-worth and value ("Contributions of Existential Psychotherapy," p. 50).

With this threat of "imminent non-being," we can live our lives always trying to elude death. Running away from death is also to run away from life. When we feel basic anxiety, we sense that death is lurking at our doorstep. We fear we will be swept away, never recover, be lost forever. We feel like a particle lost in space. We have no refuge.

The story of a little boy who was suffering a terminal illness illustrates the "stuff" of anxiety. He was asked to draw a picture that would show how he was feeling. He drew a small, attractive cottage painted white with green shutters. There were red flowers in boxes along the windows that had bright, cheery curtains. Smoke was gently wafting from the chimney. The house was set in a green yard with a well-tended garden filled with colorful flowers. Surrounded by a white picket fence, it was the picture of tranquility. Then he drew a picture of himself on a black paved road in front of the house. It was of a little boy being threatened by a huge, menacing tank that was unrelentingly moving toward him. He stood there holding up a small sign that read STOP.

When we have exhausted all possibilities and our own efforts have no effect in overcoming the oncoming menace, our powerlessness leaves us with an unfamiliar and upsetting sense of vulnerability. We must admit that we do need help. We think we should turn to others who can protect us, someone who is more powerful, more knowledgeable. We may be willing to pay any price to avoid what threatens us. We may even be willing to abandon and sacrifice part of ourselves so that we can avoid becoming isolated and alone.

Our vulnerability intensifies when pools of old anxieties arise from the past. Memories of past compromises and broken promises haunt us. Our anxiety can rise to a boiling point. We discover that the house of our life has been built on a false foundation, not our true self. We find it is made of borrowed materials. It does not come from our authentic self and talent. We become exhausted trying to hold together what we have created at the expense of our selves. We can become immobilized or suffer from anxiety attacks, psychosomatic symptoms, or illnesses.

Anxiety can lead us to capitulation by tempting us into the trap of conformism. Rollo May writes that we find conformism everywhere. It provides an escape from taking a stand and making a decision at transition times in our life. He calls conformity the tendency we have to go along with the crowd. We do not think or judge. Instead of choosing we just get swept along with the flow. Examples of conformity are familiar to us, all around us.

So much advertising appeals to and invites us to conformism. Some attract us when we are young by suggesting that we follow beautiful women or rugged men, starlets, or athletes. We ought to do what they do. These ads appeal to our dreams and vanity. Other advertising promises help to those who want to change something in their lives. The ads may appeal to those who want a cure from some physical distress or for an illness. There are others who promise safe and secure ways that lead to spiritual health: spiritual help groups that have mushroomed recently and religiously oriented groups like Buddhism, Islam, Judaism, or Christianity. Churches are a natural place to look when our life is deeply threatened. If they do not help us to live more congruently from our own deep self, the hidden self of Saint Paul, they may lead us only into conformism with a holy face. They ignore May's claim that we may become less a person. Conformism leads to a

> loss of our own identity, awareness, potentialities, individuality, i.e., whatever characterizes us as a unique and original human being. The individual temporarily escapes the anxiety of nonbeing by this means, but at the price of forfeiting his own power and sense of existence (Ibid., p. 49).

Conformity is a high price to pay to relieve our anxiety. When we try to find our identity *in* others rather than *with* another, we lose our being. We sacrifice ourselves and begin to live secondhand lives. How often, when asked who we are, do we boast about our titles, professions, relationships, or tell stories of our achievements. The question of who we are still remains unanswered. Sam Keen reminds us that at mid-life we are confronted with the realization of how much of ourselves we have buried or neglected due to conformity. We have paid tribute to Caesar, but we have neglected God and ourselves.

> The systematic diminishing of our potentiality in the socialization process sows the seeds of the crisis of adulthood—the mid-life crisis. Our membership and role in society are purchased at the cost of ignoring what is unique, idiosyncratic, amoral, antisocial, or asocial within the self (p. 123).

The crisis of anxiety that we experience during our mid-life passage brings us face to face with the life we have lived, with our choices and refusals, with roads taken and not taken. How has conformism influenced our lives? Have we chosen safety and security over living life fully and creatively? Have we hidden our talent or cultivated it? We stand before the tribunal of our hidden Self who asks us who are we, who have we become, how have we lived the life that was given to us? These questions go beyond our faults and sins. The word of God questioning us "is something alive and active: it cuts more incisively than a two-edged sword: it can seek out the place where soul is divided from spirit, or joints from marrow. It can pass judgment on secret emotions and thought" (Heb 4:12–13).

Our "word" and Spirit ask us what we have done with our life, our being, our talent, our personhood.

Thomas P. and Patrick T. Malone, father and son psychotherapists, coined the term "selficide" to describe the way most of us choose conformity and become less than we are meant to be. Selficide is a spiritual inertia to heed the command in creation to grow and come to fullness. It is a deadly aspect of conformism. It signifies a slow, often unnoticeable, process of choices not to be ourselves. They write that

> selficide describes the "leaking away" of personhood, the ways in which we make ourselves less than whole. Such a lack of wholeness is certainly far more prevalent and, in a certain sense, much more malignant than the abrupt end of life found in suicide. . . . This loss of being is the personal process wherein we injure, stunt, immobilize, damage, and deaden our *self-being*. It is actually psychological cancer, and we bring it on ourselves (p. 19).

The Malones are very explicit in showing us how to recognize "selficide" in ourselves. When we fail to continue to grow, our lives become habit rather than experience. We settle for the status quo and boredom:

> If [a person's] experiences are the same experiences, unendingly repetitious, at some point it ceases to be experience and becomes habit or personal rote. This "rigor mortis" is selficide. The person literally "lives out" their life, and there is little difference in their

experience when they are five, sixteen, forty, or seventy years old. *Self* does not emerge (Ibid., p. 7).

As with conformism, our alienation from the depths of ourselves, our hidden self, increases. Our life energy dwindles, becomes unchanging and rigid, and we die. The Malones claim that Anne Morrow Lindberg gives a vivid description of the subtlety of this kind of death. She gives us a hint to know when we do it.

> In *The Steep Ascent*, she wrote, "People 'died' all the time in their lives. Parts of them died when they made the wrong kinds of decisions—decisions against life. Sometimes they died bit by bit until finally they were just living corpses walking around. If you were perceptive you could see it in their eyes; the fire had gone out . . . but you always knew when you were making a decision against life. When you denied life you were warned. The cock crowed, always, somewhere inside you. The door clicked and you were safe inside—safe and dead" (Ibid., p. 14).

Sam Keen reminds us of the tragic results that come from choosing the safety and security of conformity or "selficide." We bury our talent and hide our self. We shut the door and turn our backs on further life and growth. He observes that:

> A majority of people in most cultures in normal times will choose to remain at home within the security of the mythic consensus and appointed roles. They will avoid

solitude, flee from self-knowledge, and remain asleep within the mutual hypnosis of the accepted social order (p. 123).

Our mid-life passage to maturity calls us to the forgiveness and healing of conversion. The Lord's promise that he has come to bring life in abundance gives us hope that we can find a true foundation for our life. Through him life opens wider at mid-life. It does not contract or remain static.

The prayer that Jesus taught us as his own prayer highlights how closely sin, evil, and, anxiety are related. The prayer that follows it in the Roman Catholic Mass highlights the crisis nature of anxiety.

> Deliver us, Lord, from every evil, and grant us peace in our day. In your mercy keep us from sin and protect us from all anxiety as we wait in joyful hope for the coming of our Savior, Jesus Christ.

Bargaining is a frequent reaction when we are besieged by anxiety. We find that we must make a choice, but we need a little more time. We need time to gather our strength to prepare ourselves for what is to come. Hoping to delay the process of this vital transition, we may look for some kind of reprieve or cure. Most bargaining shows that we are somehow aware that this is a life-or-death situation. Kübler-Ross writes that most bargaining is made with God. "In interviews, we were impressed with the number of people who made promises of a 'life dedicated to God' or a 'life of service to the Church.'" These promises are made in an attempt to postpone or alleviate the pain and the anxiety we experience. We try to appease God. We think we can turn to

God who will not reject or abandon us as others have. We then attempt to ally ourselves with him by promising to do what we think will please him.

Bargaining is not a time to make decisions, except the decision to continue the journey. We must continue to choose life even when it seems impossible. We need to remain open to what we will discover in the process, to have the readiness to be opened to change and new life. This time of exploration can purify and free us from unnecessary guilt so we can pursue our true calling in an adult and free manner.

Bargaining is a necessary stage in the development and process of the dying that is part of conversion. "A seed must die before it brings new life." Anxiety can become the threshold for entering more deeply into the kingdom of God within. When we recognize that this process, this growth which is more like death, is beyond us, we begin to meet the God within. Often we seem to have only known the God outside us and above. We need help to listen to and distinguish the many voices we hear if we will find God's will for us.

Perhaps we need to reflect on the meaning of Carl Jung's insight. It can help us to follow Jesus more closely by being inspired by him rather than imitating him. Jung reminds us of the limits of imitation. He writes that "It is no easy matter to live a life modeled on Christ's, but it is unspeakably harder to live one's own life as truly as Christ lived his!" (C. G. Jung, p. 522). Jesus' life becomes a model of inspiration, not imitation.

In anxiety it is important to remain present to our experience, to explore our desert land. Psychologist Frances Vaughan Clark advises us to develop a receptive attitude to what is occurring in our inner life. We need to admit that what we discover is part of our reality. We must learn to be non-judgmental, and not to exaggerate what we find. We need someone who will walk with us and help us to listen to the clamor of inner voices until we can hear who is calling us. We need someone who is good at:

> Helping the individual to differentiate between the true inner teacher and the many distracting solicitations of false teachers, both inner and outer. . . . This is a twofold process: First, we must learn to tune into our selves and to listen to our own inner truth. The second step is learning to trust the intuitions or inner voice which provides choices and allows us to assume responsibility of our selves (Frances Vaughan Clark, p. 76).

We need someone who has traveled a similar road. However, such people may not be easy to find. We do not need someone who has the answers, but one who can stand with us as we wait to hear God's answer. At such times we frequently turn to people of the church hoping they will be able to show us the way through this darkness. However, many clergy persons, uneasy with people who suffer from so many conflicting emotions, want to talk about God and prayer. In the name of religion, they ignore our condition. Using a subtle form of denial, they may want to follow their way of practices. That may assuage our anxiety—for a while. Usually this thin cover of piety wears thin as our anxiety and fear continue.

Anxiety becomes more difficult to bear when we experience self-assured people who seemingly sail along confidently with answers and explanations. With such sure, unquestioning confidence in their own beliefs they seem to look condescendingly at us and mock us. These men and women have often not allowed the vital questions about life and identity to stir in them. Some have resolved the problem by becoming staunch supporters of the accepted social order. They have sacrificed themselves to the group beliefs. Others use dogmatic faith to stifle the questions. Those who would speak for God may plunge us more deeply into the darkness of despair. Unfortunately both groups stifle the voice of the living God.

Psychologists or psychiatrists are frequently called in to help us deal with extreme anxiety. Such action often further deepens our feelings of being lost and helpless. It makes us feel we are outside of or beyond God's help. It may help to deepen the divide between the human and the spiritual. The religious is praised as if from God and the human is disparaged as if it were not. We may feel totally beyond help.

We must not make a vow or a promise while we are in anxiety. It is not yet time for that. Above all we must not look for someone who affirms and spiritualizes our promises of denial. They do not promote greater and more faithful incarnate living. We must remember the words of the author of Hebrews (Heb 10:5-7) when he explains the verses of Psalm 40:6–8: "You who wanted no sacrifice or oblation prepared a body for me. You took no pleasure in holocausts or sacrifices for sin; then I said, just as I was commanded in the scroll of the book, "God, here I am! I am coming to obey your will." The author says that Jesus is abolishing the first in order to establish the second that brings life in abundance and will make us holy. In other words, we are growing beyond the limitations of our early lives to begin to live wholly in abundance of life.

The real danger of spiritualizing "bargaining" is that it brings on the death we are trying to avoid. Sam Keen warns us:

> Abandon the quest for your unique self and you will live with the fear that others will abandon you. Your infantile shame will become permanent because your unexplored self will be embarrassed in the presence of the facade you have created (p. 125)!

In bargaining, we tend to say "Yes," to ally ourselves with others. We have a tendency to stand with the other, to cling for security. The great danger in bargaining is that we sell our selves to follow the path of least resistance. We enter into an inertia of spirit, into stagnation. If we have not cut off or short-circuited the process by conformism or selficide, we next begin to move away, to move within. We must learn to say goodbye.

As sadness and grieving overwhelm us as the spiral downward and inward continues, we experience our helplessness, our inability even "to be." Powerlessness showed us we were not able to act, to do, to stop what was happening. Helplessness affects our being itself. It brings us close to death. We learn the true poverty and littleness of our spirit; the actuality of being nothing. We experience ourselves as abandoned, narrowed, and caught in a small space. We feel sterile, barren, numb, in utter darkness, utter emptiness, on the edge of despair and hopelessness. Perhaps the words of the psalmist speaks of our condition: "You have turned my friends and neighbors against me, now darkness is my one companion left" (Ps 88:18).

Thomas Merton shows the fierceness of the battle that brings on this condition. He calls it "the most terrible of all wars."

> This battle of life and death goes on in us inexorably and without mercy. If we become aware of it above all in our spirit, we find ourselves involved in a terrible wrestling not of questions and answers, but of being and nothingness, spirit and void. In this most terrible of all wars, fought on the brink of infinite despair, we come gradually to realize that life is more than the reward for one who correctly guesses a secret and spiritual "answer" (p. 3).

Sadness and grief uncover underlying feelings of helplessness, barrenness, and sterility, our true poverty of spirit. In grieving there is a great sense of loss and inner pain. We feel that we are losing a familiar and valuable part of ourselves, one who has helped us to weave the fabric of our lives. It may be someone we have loved. Or it may be our faith, idealism, good deeds, service, or our love.

We find a good example in Saint Peter. The same strength that allowed him to be bold and a leader in following Jesus needed to be purified. The Father had gifted him to say that Jesus was indeed the Christ. Even Jesus had promised that he was to be the Rock on which his church would be built. But Peter's very strength, boldness, and faith had to be purified if he was to be a rock of support rather than a stumbling block to his brothers and sisters. Then he could become the confessor on whom and with whom others could find their own true faith. Jesus prayed for him that he would recover and strengthen his brothers.

We need people to pray for us that we too may grow through our pain and suffering.

We must also lose those gifts which have helped to weave the fabric of our faith life so they can be transformed into adult and living faith, hope, and love. Those gifts have brought us to this place of conversion. Perhaps the human form of these gifts must become divinized by God's gracious hand.

But God has seemed to forsake us. We may feel he has abandoned us. We can appreciate Jesus' sob in the Garden crying out his abandonment. Our reaction can be either a withdrawn capitulation into a stubborn helplessness, or it can signal a moving within to allow new growth to germinate. We also remember Jesus' admonition to the apostles that he must go away so the Spirit of Jesus could come to heal and teach them. Jesus had forgiven them; the Spirit would heal them and remain with them to teach and bring them to the fullness of life. Our tears of sadness water the roots of new life. God calls us to stand alone, but not in isolation. This absence facilitates our growing out of a childish dependence on God so that we may become the sons and daughters of God.

We may have some guilt or shame during this time of our helplessness and grief. We do not understand what is happening in us and we fear others will not understand. This feeling is often reinforced and exacerbated when others misinterpret this dynamic of the conversion process. Our suffering may increase when they judge us as being a burden, for being non-productive, for becoming non-functional. They add to our suffering when they say our faith is weak. We all must remember that suffering is the school and foundation of the hope that is not deceptive. Saint Paul writes: "Sufferings bring patience, as we know, and patience brings perseverance, perseverance brings hope, and this hope is not deceptive, because the love of God has been poured into our hearts by the Holy Spirit" (Rom 5:3–6).

Kübler-Ross describes two kinds of grieving. They are very different in nature and should be recognized as such. One needs to remember, to touch, to talk. The other wants to be quiet, silent, and waiting. Both have their place in the process.

A friend diagnosed with breast cancer had a radical mastectomy. With her body unable to receive chemotherapy her future looked very bleak. Although we were friends I could not be present to her in the same way as someone who had a similar experience. After some time she met a terminally ill medical doctor who had started a movement called "One Day at a Time!" Periodically she would call him so they could talk. One day, filled with sadness and grief, she came to see me. She had called her friend only to be told by his wife that he had died. She was filled with grief at losing this friend, but at the same time she was feeling her own grief at her impending death. Thankfully, she is still alive twenty years later.

In reactive grieving we feel a great sense of loss and sorrow at losing everything and everyone we have loved. We need to say "goodbye," to bid farewell. There is the need to spend time with, to talk with, to touch all that has been part of our life. In this grieving, we need to talk. We need someone who can be with us to listen.

A friend whose sister was dying of cancer was called to her home at the end. His sister had spent time saying goodbye to the house she had planned with her husband, to the furniture and furnishings she had so carefully picked out. She walked around her house to touch the plants, trees, and flowers she tended so carefully. Filled with memories, she spent time talking with her children and her husband. She had touched them all, remembered details, talked with them. She was more ready to leave.

We must learn to say "goodbye." It is not easy for anyone. We have been conditioned to let go, to cut off, to turn and walk away. No goodbyes! Many organizations abruptly move families with much less care and concern than is taken in transplanting a tree. In transplanting a tree you carry some of the old familiar soil with you. You carefully prepare the new ground. After transplanting you tend carefully to watering and mulching until the tree's roots are firmly held and growing. The sorrow and sadness of saying "goodbye" is not self-pity.

We have many tears to cry. Pools of tears are waiting to be cried. All the losses, sadness, and grief that have not been expressed in the past are still alive in us. They need to speak their unspoken words and cry their tears. We ought not be ashamed of the freeing tears that arise from our depths. We need to lament; we have need for "days of lamentation." A significant sign of conversion for Saint Ignatius Loyola and early church fathers was uncontrollable crying of stored up tears that are released in deep forgiveness.

Preparatory grief and quiet interweave our saying "goodbye." We are preparing for our final impending change. This is a time of silent grief as we leave behind so much that has been part of our lives. There is little or no need for many words, for talking. But, we do need someone to be with us, to stay with us. "Watch with me!" We are sad. Even though we may feel ready and even be eager to end this turmoil, it is not yet God's time. This is a time of great activity on God's part as he prepares a place for us and himself within us. Our waiting can become holy and a source of grace. We are waiting for a coming home to ourselves and to God. Our waiting is not with fear or anxiety. It is waiting for God. And he will come.

Chapter 6

HOPE IN DARKNESS

In the dying process of conversion, life and death are at war within us. What is alive in us needs to be refined; what is dead needs to be wakened and accepted into life. What is still to come must be born. "Everything hangs on the final issue, in the battle of life and death. Nothing is assured beforehand" (Merton, p. 4). This uncertainty leads us to the agony, the darkness where we cannot be sure of our own choices. Are we strong enough to continue choosing life and love when to live means to go on and on with this absurd battle of being and becoming?

Thomas Merton reminds us, "The roots of life remain immortal and alive in us if we will continue to keep morally alive" (p. 4). Likewise, Elisabeth Kübler-Ross found that hope runs like a living stream through the valleys of dying and being born again. A thread of hope interweaves our losses. Kübler-Ross writes that

> The one thing that usually persists through all these stages is hope. In listening to our terminally ill patients we were always impressed that even the most accepting, the most realistic patients left the possibility open for some cure, for the discovery of a new

drug, or the "last minute" success in a research project. . . . It is this glimpse of hope which maintains them through their suffering. It is the feeling that all this must have some meaning, will pay off eventually, that they can endure it for a little while longer . . . it gives the terminally ill a sense of a mission in life which helps them to maintain their spirits. They showed the greatest confidence in the doctors who allowed for such hope. If the patient stops expressing hope, it is usually a sign of imminent death (pp. 138–140).

These observations by Kübler-Ross direct our attention to the experience and dynamic of hope. If we reflect on this hope, it is found in the same place where we find no escape from the pain, the suffering, and the seeming end of our journey. In these straits we may try to deny, lie about, or distance ourselves from what is happening. We do so at our own peril. Suffering itself forces us to be present to what is going on, and to ourselves. We begin to have a sense that this is not just some accidental torment that we are suffering. It will have some meaning, some pay off. After some time we feel a sense of purpose or mission, if not for ourselves, then for others.

But we only have a glimpse of hope. "Hope, in its full supernatural dimension is beyond our power and when we try to keep ourselves in hope by sheer violent persistence in willing to live, we end if not in despair but in what is worse—delusion" (Merton, p. 4).

Merton insists that we discover hope when we enter the depths of our helplessness. He reminds us that it is a gift. It is not the reward for our heroic efforts or our goodness that we earn or merit it.

> Hope then is a gift. It springs out of nothingness, completely free. But to meet it, we have to descend into nothingness, and there we meet hope most perfectly, when we are stripped of our own confidence. "A hope that is seen," says St. Paul, "is no hope, therefore despair, to see your hope is to abandon hope" (Ibid., pp. 4–5).

We meet hope at our limits where we fear we can no longer survive or go on. We feel alone and abandoned. We are very close to despair.

> The truth is that there can strictly speaking be no hope except when the temptation to despair exists. Hope is the act by which this temptation is actively or victoriously overcome. The victory may not invariably involve any sense of effort: I should even be quite ready to go so far as to say that such a feeling is not compatible with hope in its purest form (Gabriel Marcel, p. 36).

Upon reflection we begin to realize that we find the basis of our hope in the many ways God has entered our lives in the past. He has been faithful to us from the beginning, despite our infidelity. We can begin to understand the basis of our hope against the background of the Hebrew scriptures where hope is expressed as "waiting for, being expectant, wait longingly." This Old Testament hope was based on the experience of God's faithfulness and promises amidst the successes and failure of Israel's history.

New Testament hope is based on God's manifestation of himself and his faithfulness to us in his Son, Jesus of Nazareth. Hope does not try to determine how God will show himself, but remains open for all God's new and astonishing manifestations of love. It encourages us on our journey when we rely on Jesus' continuing assurance that he will be with us.

Evelyn Underhill shows how hope continues both to purify us and ready us for continuing the journey of our life. "Hope is supremely the virtue of the incomplete (not the deficient); of the creature stretching out beyond present boundaries toward life and love—toward God and His Spirit poured into us" (p. 64). God does not remove our burdens, but they become easier to bear.

> The old moralists said that Hope was the virtue which purified memory and made it fit for God; and by memory they meant all our funded experience, the hoarded past which we drag along with us. Hope teaches us the art of wise forgetting; of dropping the superfluous, the outgrown, the trivial. It cleanses the mind and lifts up all the rest of our experience into the eternal light saying: "Even though I do not see the meaning, yet I know all this is conditioning my growth, purifying my spirit, taking me towards You" (Ibid., p. 62–63).

Hope helps us to be free of petty and narrow concerns. It expands our vision and allows us to begin to see our lives through the eyes of and in the perspective of love, both our own loves and eventually God's love which was so great that he sent his son to be Jesus of Nazareth.

> Hope finds all life penetrated by a
> significance that points beyond itself, and has
> a trustful expectation that the ceaseless
> stream of events, thoughts, joys, trials means
> something, contributes to something; and
> only has value because it points beyond itself
> to God, is an earnest of rich fields of
> experience awaiting us (Ibid., p. 63).

This kind of hope, learned again and again in the stubble fields of our lives, teaches us something of God's providence. It helps us to find God in all things. This hope allowed the apostles to let go of their own preconceptions that they learned from their experiences of Jesus himself. It seemed they thought at first that faith in Christ was only for the people of Israel. Their surprising experience that even Cornelius, the Roman, was given the same Spirit that they had received changed their whole outlook. It allowed them to be men who could admit they could make mistakes, did not understand. They learned that God could still teach them. Even God can be in our mistakes. Underhill affirms that "Hope is supremely the virtue of the incomplete (not the deficient); of the creature stretching out beyond present boundaries toward life and love, care and truth—toward God and His Spirit poured into us" (p. 64).

Hope not only sustains us through suffering and helplessness, it allows us to experience the true purpose and meaning of our lives. Hope does not bind us to God in order to do his will slavishly. It frees us find new ways to fulfill our unique vocation to share God's life and love with others. In this way we do God's will. We fulfill his hope for us and the world.

For the true basis of our hope of God is God's hope for us. . . . He has made us for Himself; but the fulfillment of that hope is partly in our own hands. When we think of this aspect of our freedom—that there is one fragment of the Eternal purpose which no one else can fulfill, one place in the world where we and none other are meant to transmit God's life and love, and so fulfill His Hope—then even in our timid souls there is born a faint desire to give ourselves without reserve to His purpose, whatever the cost. There is work which God requires to be done by each one of us, and which no one else can do (Ibid., pp. 70–71).

In Saint Paul we learn that the reality of hope is to choose life and love in the midst of abandonment and failure. It is not choosing life by ignoring the dying that is diminishing us nor a life in the future. We are enabled to accept the life, though unseen, that is present in our limited situations. Hope has to do with choosing to live and to love, while giving birth to new life.

From the beginning till now the entire creation, as we know, has been groaning in one great act of giving birth; and not only creation, but all of us who possess the first-fruits of the SPIRIT, we too groan inwardly as we wait for our bodies to be set free. For we must be content to hope that we shall be saved—our salvation is not in sight, we should not have to be hoping for it if it were—but, as I say, we must hope to be saved since we are not saved yet, it is something we must wait for with patience (Rom 8:23–25).

The power of Jesus' resurrection moved Paul in his desire to know, *connaître*, i.e., to be born with Christ. The pattern of Jesus' death was to live a life of loving even when it brought suffering. He prays: "All I want is to know Christ and the power of his resurrection and to share his sufferings by reproducing the pattern of his death. That is the way I can hope to take my place in the resurrection of the dead. I have not won . . . let us go forward on the road that has brought us to where we are" (Phil 3:10–17).

We learn that suffering is a school of pruning and purgation. It teaches us patience. We learn not to run away. This patience fosters perseverance. Together they lead to a hope that is not in vain. Brother David Steindl-Rast sheds wise light on the nature of purgation.

> This process of purgation is at the core of every spiritual discipline. Patience holds still in the blast-furnace of experience. Discipline is not so much a matter of doing this or that, but of holding still. Not as if this would cost no effort. But the effort is all applied to the crucial tasks, the task of making no effort.

In the poetry of T.S. Eliot's *Four Quartets*:

> I said to my soul, be still, and wait without hope
>
> For hope would be hope for the wrong thing; wait without love
>
> For love would be love for the wrong thing; there is yet faith

> But the faith and the hope and the love are
> all in the waiting,

The disciple waiting on the master is silent. The pupil, eye-to-eye with the teacher, is all attention. This stillness is not a shutting up. It is the stillness of the anemone wide open to the sunlight. Even the clatter of thoughts is silenced by the discipline of stillness. Says Eliot:

> Wait without thought, for you are not
> ready for thought:

> So the darkness shall be light and the
> stillness the dancing.

The Dance Master of spiritual discipline is a most demanding teacher. The stillness and the darkness in which hope is purified is a "condition of complete simplicity/(costing not less than everything)" (p. 137).

Both Saint Paul and Eliot stress an essential aspect of hope: waiting. Most of us are too impatient to wait when we are young. As we grow old we tend to wonder what is left that is worth waiting for. But somewhere between superficial optimism and cynical pessimism lies the youthful dance of hope, graceful in its stillness. We have learned how to wait in total attention for each new possibility of life, for each new surprise of our amazing God. Samuel Beckett focuses our attention on the waiting that brings care and hope.

In *Waiting for Godot*, it is of the essence that Godot does not come. We wait forever and the problem remains. Beckett shocks us into the awareness of our human significance, forcing us to look more deeply into our condition as men and women. We find ourselves caring despite the apparent meaninglessness of the situation. Godot does not come, but in the waiting there is care and hope. It matters that we, like characters in the drama, wait and that we wait in human relationship. Waiting is caring and caring is hoping (Rollo May, *Love and Will*, p. 305).

In hope we wait for God's time, not our own. We wait for the surprising manifestation that cuts across our expectations, but brings meaning to all the lines of our life. Like the Holy Spirit, hope is not seen, but it makes itself known in a powerful way that inflames and illumines us. It is the carrier of God's gifts. It is the bridge that leads to healing the opposites within us. Hope brings back a youthfulness that we lost many years ago when, out of fear, we quit hoping. Joseph Pieper, a well-known writer about hope, claims that if we have learned the virtue of hope we radiate an unexpected youthfulness. "Therefore, we do not grow faint," Saint Paul writes, "even though outwardly we wear out, inwardly we grow younger day by day" (2 Cor 4:16).

Chapter 7

SUFFERING AND ACCEPTANCE

As the cancer of spirit at mid-life unrelentingly attacks us, the experiences of the terminally ill speak to our condition. When the anxiety and suffering continue without relief, questions plague us. Why would a good and just God allow people to suffer? Does any good come out of suffering? What value does suffering have? They are asked every day and have been asked down the ages. We are brought up against the mystery of a God who proclaims justice and love while he does not rescue even a good man from suffering.

The book of Job in the Hebrew scriptures recounts very vividly the classic story of a man who asked God questions about suffering and demanded answers. In dramatic fashion, it presents opposing attitudes toward suffering. It highlights a common belief that suffering is just punishment for our sin, contrasting Job who calls himself "innocent" with his friends who declare that God will find Job "guilty." On the one hand, Job admits that he has sinned, but insists he is not guilty of committing evil by victimizing others or himself. He continues to protest his innocence while he laments his terrible fate. He struggles mightily to understand why God is testing him by allowing him to suffer. On the other hand, we find Job's friends who come to offer him their support. They confidently defend the belief that suffering is in retribution for guilt. If Job suffers, it is because he has sinned. They assure him that the all-powerful God will not pardon him even if Job thinks that God already has forgiven him.

The story begins: "There was a man called Job: a sound and honest man who feared God and shunned evil" (Jb 1:1). He is a man who has a large family and vast possessions. He is well-respected by his peers. One day God approaches Satan and asks him whether he knows his faithful servant, Job. Satan says he does, but adds that Job is faithful to God because he has been so blessed. Satan challenges God to take away Job's family and possessions, then "I warrant you, he will curse you to your face" (Jb 1:12). God tells Satan that he accepts his challenge. "All he has is in your power. But keep your hands off his person" (Jb 1:12).

Satan sees to it that one by one Job loses his children as well as his possessions. Job tears his gown and shaves his head, but perseveres in faith. He says, "Naked I came from my mother's womb, naked shall I return, Blessed be the name of Yahweh" (Jb 1:21). God boasts to Satan that he has provoked Job to no avail. Satan replies that a man will give all he has to save his life but "lay a finger on his bone and flesh; I warrant you he will curse you to your face." Again God grants Satan his challenge, saying, "he is in your power, but spare his life." Thus "Job was struck down with malignant ulcers from the sole of his feet to the top of his head" (Jb 2:6–7).

Job's faithfulness to God does not prevent him from complaining. He curses the day he was conceived, asking why he was born at all. He asks, "Why me," and laments, "If only things had been different!" He complains: "Lying in bed I wonder, 'When will it be day?' Risen I think 'How slowly evening comes?' Restlessly I fret till twilight falls. Vermin and loathsome scabs cover my body; my skin is cracked and oozes pus" (Jb 7:4–5). He comes close to despair, asking whether all help has deserted him. "Will no one hear my prayer, will not God himself grant my hope? May it please God to crush me, to give his hand free play and do away with me! Have I the strength to go on waiting" (Jb 6:8–9).

As his suffering continues and his faith in God brings him no respite, Job continues to cry out and complain.

> Now I am the laughing-stock of my juniors, the young people, whose fathers I did not consider fit to put with the dogs who looked after my flocks (Jb 30:1).

> To them I am loathsome, they stand aloof from me, do not scruple to spit on me (Jb 30:21).

> Terrors turn to meet me, my confidence is blown away as if by the wind, my hope of safety passes like a cloud (Jb 30:15).

> I cry to you and you give me no answer; I stand before you, but you take no notice. You have grown cruel in your dealings with me, your hand lies on me, heavy and hostile (Jb 30:20–21).

Then his friends who come to support him unwittingly add to his suffering when they tell him that he deserves this punishment. They taunt him by saying "now your turn has come, and you lose patience, at the first touch on yourself you are overwhelmed. . . . I speak from experience: those who plough iniquity and sow disaster reap just that" (Jb 4:5). Feeling the weight of his friends' condemnation, but still hoping in God's great mercy, Job, close to despair, cries out:

> There is always hope for a tree: when felled, it can start its life again; its shoots continue to sprout. Its roots may have grown old in the earth, its stump rotting in the ground, but let it scent the water, and it buds, and puts out branches like a plant newly set. But a human being? He dies, and dead he remains, breathes his last, and then where is he? A human being, once laid to rest, will never rise again (Jb 14:7–12).

Job's faith in God remains alive even in the face of his own suffering and the discouraging arguments of his friends who say that God judges him guilty. But Job proclaims his innocence:

> I swear by the living God who denies me justice, by Shaddai who has turned my life sour, that as long as a shred of life is left in me, my lips shall never speak untruth nor any lie be found on my tongue. Far from ever admitting you to be right, I will maintain my innocence to my dying day. I take my stand on my integrity, I will not stir. My conscience gives me no cause to blush for my life (Jb 27:1–6).

Interspersed with his complaints and lamentation over his misfortune and deathly condition, we hear Job cry out his conviction that God will not desert him. In fact it seems that as his fate grows worse his belief in the goodness of God grows stronger.

> Will no one let my words be recorded, inscribed with iron chisel and engraving tool, cut in the rock for ever? I know that my Defender lives and that he will take his stand on earth. After my awakening He will set me close to him, and from my flesh I shall look on God. He whom I shall see will take my part: my eyes will be gazing on no stranger (Jb 19:23–27).

At last God breaks in on the dialog between Job and his so-called friends. He turns to one of them and says: "I burn with anger against you and your friends for not speaking truthfully about me as my servant Job has done" (Jb 41:7–8). In turn God also confronts Job. "Brace yourself like a fighter, now it is my turn to ask questions and yours to inform me" (Jb 40:7). Then God asks Job where he was when the world and all things in it were created. He asks him about times and seasons. He asks whether the strong and powerful on the earth can compare with God. He asks about the power and wisdom of God. Humbled, but not overwhelmed, Job acknowledges who God is. He has come to know him in a new and personal way, not in a slavish way.

> This was the answer Job gave to Yahweh: I knew that you are all-powerful; what you can conceive you can perform. I am the man who obscured your designs with empty-headed words. . . . I knew you then only by hearsay; but now, having seen you with my own eyes, I retract all I have said and in dust and ashes I repent (Jb 42:3–6).

A note in the Jerusalem Bible says this was not strictly speaking of a vision, but a fresh appreciation of the true nature of God.

> Job's questions about his suffering have not been answered, but he has come to understand that God's wisdom may give an unsuspected meaning to such realities as suffering, sin, and death (*The Jerusalem Bible*, p. 777).

The book of Job states very clearly that Job grew through his suffering. He came to know God, "having seen him with his own eyes." God condemned Job's false comforters who stayed away at a safe distance from Job's pain and suffering. They presumed to speak in God's name. They used the scriptures and teaching of rabbis to try to bring Job to repentance. To Job, suffering but innocent, God gave no answer to his questions or explanation for his suffering. God showed that he is and has been present by revealing himself in his infinite power and glory. The effect for Job was to experience that everything, no matter how dark and painful, has meaning.

Perhaps Psalm 51, the *Miserere*, best captures the spirit of these reflections. It points out that God does not ask for sacrifices and holocausts. A broken spirit is sacrifice enough.

> Save me from death, God my savior,
>   and my tongue will acclaim your
>   righteousness;
> Lord, open my lips,
> and my mouth will speak out your praise.
> Sacrifice gives you no pleasure,

were I to offer holocaust, you would not have
    it.
My sacrifice is this broken spirit,
You will not scorn this crushed and broken
    heart. (Ps 51:14–17).

These words remind us of God's command in creation. Repeatedly he calls us to life, to become fecund and fruitful. Job's story reminds us that sin, suffering, and death entered our world with the sin of Adam. God did not punish Adam for his sin. But he let him taste what he had chosen to eat, the fruit of the tree of knowledge of good and evil. God respects our freedom, the choices we make even when they do not bring life.

From our earliest days God exhorts us to choose life. "I set before you life or death, blessing or curse. Choose life!" (Dt 30:19). We know we must choose, but we do not know what choice will bring life or death, blessing or curse. We need to learn this through experience. We come in time to discover that some of our choices have not brought life. They have given rise to sin and uncovered roots of sinfulness within us.

We find God's amazing response to our sinfulness in the book of Wisdom. We find hope in the way that God deals with our sin and unfaithfulness. He has a heart for our misery.

> You are merciful to all, because you can do all things and overlook men's sins so they can repent. Yes, you love all that exists, you hold nothing of what you have made in abhorrence. . . . You spare all things because all things are yours, Lord, lover of life, you whose imperishable spirit is in all. Little by

> little, therefore, you correct those who offend,
> you admonish and remind them of how they
> have sinned, so that they may abstain from
> evil and trust in you, Lord (Wis 11:24–12:2).

When we, on our part, recognize that we have sinned we think that God will punish us. Out of fear we try to avoid punishment by making sacrifices that will appease God. The psalmist tells us that God's ways are different from ours. God does not want sin offerings, but wants us to do God's will, which is to choose life, not death. He writes:

> You wanted no sacrifice or cereal offering, but
> you gave me an open ear [literally, you dug
> out my ear], you did not ask for burnt
> offerings or sacrifice for sin; then I said, "Here
> I am, I am coming." In the scroll of the book
> it is written of me, my delight is to do your
> will; your law, my God, is deep in my heart
> (Ps 40:6–8).

God does not will or intend our suffering in any way. He does not tell us to choose suffering. In fact, he is not pleased with sacrifices. His only desire for us is that we choose life and love. "For it is love I desire, not sacrifice, and knowledge of God rather than holocausts" (Hos 6:6). When we choose life and love we are most like God. We also know that, if we make that choice, we will know the passion and suffering that accompany them. It will not be a suffering of our own making, one that that brings death. It will be the liberating suffering of love that brings life. "To love is to live according to his commandments: this is the commandment which you have learned from the beginning, to live a life of love" (2 Jn 6).

God's response to our unfaithfulness is to show that his love is deeper and broader than our suffering and sinfulness. "Because this people approaches me only in words, honors me only with lip service while their hearts are far from me. . . . I shall have to go on astounding this people by being prodigal of prodigious prodigies" (Is 29:13–14).

The author of the letter to the Hebrews uses the same words of Psalm 40 to tell us that God does not want sacrifice. He introduces a radically new view of suffering by stating that God took flesh in Jesus and that living our own incarnation is the way to find God's will. "You [God] wanted no sacrifice or cereal offerings; but you gave me a body. You took no pleasure in burnt offerings or sacrifices for sin; then I said, 'Here I am, I am coming.' In the scroll of the book is written of me to do your will, God" (Heb 10:5–7).

God shows his tremendous respect and love for us by sending his Son to live our human life. Jesus of Nazareth, a man completely like us in all things, is the climax of God's prodigious prodigies. The "mystery of the heights and depths of love" is the lesson God wants to reveal to us in his Son. God sends him to manifest the Father's love for us through his life and teaching about the Kingdom of God to which he was faithful to the end. He was faithful in love to his father and his friends even at the cost of suffering and death. His passion for life and love, loving beyond limit, brought him suffering and death at the hands of those who are afraid to love. They preferred the security of law over the living word of God and the risk of love. His completely human life gives suffering and death meaning.

Jesus' words to the Pharisees affirm again that God does not demand sacrifice. "Those who are well do not need a physician, but the sick do. Go and learn the meaning of the words 'I desire mercy, not sacrifice.' I did not come to call the righteous but sinners" (Mt 9:12–13). Jesus' mission of becoming human in every way like us was to free us from living our whole lives in slavery to the fear of death. The fear of death is the fear of entering life as God has created it. It is the fear of living incarnately. We fear the vulnerability of living as a man or woman who has to learn in the process of experience, especially affective, bodily experience; in a body destined to die.

Louis Evely, a French priest, insists that when Jesus of Nazareth suffered he was not the sacrificial victim of a demanding God, but the faithful son of a passionately loving God.

> It is not a question of suffering, but of loving. Only love, being what is divine in the world, is, like God, universal, communicable, and efficacious. The nobleness of Christ's passion is that it was not a work of asceticism, a sought-after mortification, but merely the faithfulness of love. To accept and to offer inevitable sufferings is to love God's will. To impose on ourselves voluntary sufferings is to do our will and be reassured at small cost. Your crosses must come from your commitments and not from your personal fabrication (Louis Evely, p. 31).

Life and suffering are intimately linked and bound together. Suffering is not a problem to be solved. It is mystery to be lived into. We see a "glimpse" of the mystery of God's love and respect for us. This glimpse shows how he cares for us and interacts with us from birth. He is a living and loving God. He desires that each of us arrive at the fullness of life and love.

Suffering helps us to begin to taste the passion and disorder in ourselves from the choices we have made. We can feel our distance and alienation from God. Becoming aware of our disorder and sins, we can recognize our need for freedom from fear and these constraints. We can freely turn to God to ask for his forgiveness and healing so we can enjoy the fullness of life.

Suffering and pain are part of the process of healing us where we are wounded. They heal our blindness so we can see with a heart of faith. They calm our fears and lead us to the liberation of forgiveness from our sins. Jeremiah assures us that Yahweh promises: "I will forgive their iniquity and never call their sin to mind" (Jer 30:34). By our wounds we are healed.

Suffering also is part of the process of hollowing our hearts. It opens us up and out, expanding us beyond our narrow boundaries toward completeness and compassion. In this way suffering dissipates our defensive inertia which moves us toward staying settled, secure, and safe. These lead to "selficide," the slow death we suffer by refusing to choose life. Suffering provides the space to grow into abundance in faith and hope and love.

Suffering is a means that God uses to help us know ourselves. Its penetrating light unmasks us. It exposes the lies and deceptions we use to camouflage ourselves. The author of the letter to the Hebrews tells us that "The word of God is something alive and active: . . . it can judge the secret emotions and thoughts. No created thing can hide from him; everything is uncovered and open" (Heb 4:12–13). This is not meant to bring fear. It helps us to face with honesty who we have become. We come to experience our God-given dignity as well. In self-knowledge we know and experience God as well as ourselves.

In the self-knowledge arising out of suffering, we experience God's love for us. It helps us to understand something of the gift of Jesus' human life. God did not exempt, save, or rescue Jesus from the suffering that is part of life. Jesus did not rescue or exempt his closest friends from the suffering and pain they were about to endure in his passion and death. He did not rescue them from the suffering of facing the humiliating truth about themselves in their denials and desertions. But he did pray for them. In the same way we are not exempt from the suffering that is part of life, but he gives us his Spirit.

In the story of the disciples on the way to Emmaus, once Jesus explained to his friends the necessity of suffering, their hearts were burning within them. Perhaps we all need to have this Emmaus experience when in the midst of disillusionment and discouragement Jesus tells us personally about the necessity of his suffering and that our personal suffering is not in vain. It is not punishment. We need to learn that suffering is a school in which to learn wisdom and hope, a hope that is not deceptive because it is poured into our hearts by the Spirit of Jesus.

Suffering brings wisdom, a wisdom of God, that is the path to our true, hidden Self. Once we find acceptance for our suffering, its sting is gone! Discovering that our Self can only be realized through suffering, we realize that allowing the pain and suffering, already present in our body, to enter and knead our spirit is the beginning step on the path to one's Self and to God.

In his letter to the Romans, Saint Paul points out the close relationship between suffering and a hope that is not false. He traces the progression that we ourselves may experience. In suffering we learn patience and perseverance. These lead to hope that is not deceptive.

> We can boast in our sufferings. These sufferings bring patience, as we know, and patience brings perseverance, and perseverance brings hope, and this hope is not deceptive, because the love of God has been poured into our hearts by the Holy Spirit (Rom 5:3–6).

The hope that arises out of suffering affords us a new vantage point from which we can ask questions. The focus broadens from being centered on our selves in isolation with our suffering, to how God is active and present in our suffering. We can see how God views suffering.

When, like Job, we see suffering with the eyes of hope, we recognize suffering as a blessing and a gift because it has a meaning and a definite purpose. Human suffering finds meaning in Jesus of Nazareth. In Jesus God emptied himself to become completely human. When he emptied himself completely in his suffering and death, he won victory over them. Now life is changed, not taken away or destroyed.

When suffering breaks through the wall of our personal world and exposes us to the pain and darkness of life itself, we experience our emptiness. When like Jesus we are emptied and cry out, "My God, my God, why have You forsaken me?" we may finally come to be filled with the utter wholeness of God himself. The exposed vulnerability of our wound is the door through which God enters our life.

Perhaps these words from the Japanese scientist, Takashi Nagai, best illustrate what he learned in his experience of emptiness. They can inspire us in our sufferings. They can teach all who would minister to those who suffer. Dr. Nagai was a pioneer in radiology in Nagasaki. Because of his pioneering efforts he contracted leukemia which brought on his death, but not before his wife had been killed in the atomic bomb explosion. He wrote:

> Unless you have suffered and wept you really don't understand what compassion is, nor can you give comfort to someone who is suffering. If you haven't cried you can't dry another's eyes. Unless you've walked in darkness you can't help wanderers find the way. Unless you've looked into the eyes of menacing death and felt its hot breath you can't help another rise from the dead and taste anew the joy at being alive (Takashi Nagai).

During the sadness of saying goodbye and waiting for relief from our suffering we begin to notice a change slowly and quietly taking place deep within us. Our grieving seems to recede. A calm peace filters in and gradually fills us. There is no further need for us to strive anymore, to merit or earn God's approval by our efforts. To our amazement we find an "Amen," so let it be, to this deep process of conversion, of dying, rising from within. Our yes is neither the "will-full" yes of a stoic or a "will-less" capitulation of someone resigned to his fate. It seems to arise out of our center.

On reflection we recognize with amazement the truth of Saint Paul's prayer in Ephesians. He prayed to the Father, "whose power working in us can do infinitely more than we can ask for or imagine" (Eph 3:15). We find that our "hidden self" has been strengthened. The Father has anchored us.

Christ is living in our hearts through faith. We find that our "Self" has accepted our life as it is, as it has been, and how it will be. We can only affirm with peace the acceptance of our life that we discover rising within us. We are "all right." We are ready for the next step. Somehow we know that God is present; that he always has been and will be present. We sense that everything happening to us is as it should be. We are born again. May his will be done.

This lesson was brought home to me very powerfully and personally. Standing by the bedside of my father who was dying of cancer, I was sobbing. He showed the ravages of the disease and did not have long to live. He quietly looked up at me and with a peaceful voice said "It's all right, son." He was at peace with his dying. It has taken me years to understand.

I pray that the words of Pedro Arrupe, the well-known general of the Jesuits and a man full of hope, were his too. I pray that it is ours also: "May my last Amen be my first Alleluia."

Chapter 8

BEING LED WITHIN

I have tried to describe the recurring cycle of affective changes that accompany our lives from our first cries of discomfort as an infant through our final days. At mid-life, during conversion times, these changes occur with greater intensity and at ever deepening levels. They spiral down to our depths where we find our hidden Self and meet God in Jesus of Nazareth. We need to let our feelings and emotions move us and work on us as yeast does to dough. We should not rationalize or sublimate them. We do not need those who would take away our confusion and pain in order to rescue us for God. They are liable to send us into what Viktor Frankl calls an ecclesiogenic neurosis or the deadening piety of the "noble" sufferer. We need to find companions who know the ways of affective conversion. Above all, we must try to find the faith, already present, which makes us whole, as Jesus so frequently told those who came to him for healing.

Finding words to articulate our experience can be very helpful. When we hear that our experience has a name, we can bring it into the light. We find we are not alone. We can begin to find meaning for what is happening, even if it does not stop the suffering. Bringing our experience into the light lets us breathe. It allows us to let the experience enter our spirit to change us.

On the other hand, when some people find names that describe their experience, they use words as a defense against it rather than allowing what is happening to touch them. They bury the experience and insulate themselves from letting it change them. They become "makers of speeches," as Gabriel Marcel characterizes optimists, or stoical pessimists. They keep others away with their words. They "talk the talk, but do not walk the walk." They seem unable to let Jesus' consoling promise "Fear not, I will be with you" encourage them.

These affective experiences signal an earthquake. Our conscious control loosens and we become vulnerable. The kind of person we are is revealed. These experiences lead us deeper into our selves and back to our story. We are led into a foreign land that surrounds us, but is also within us. We feel a stranger to ourselves and find strangers in ourselves whom we do not recognize.

When we enter the unknown land of our self, we find the "I," myself, who makes choices, tells my story, and remembers parts of my history. At the same time "I" disclaim or disown other parts of myself. We misspeak or commit a faux pas. We have frightening dreams. We say, "That's not me." To help us understand we must reflect on this process of being led within and back; we must consider both our "I" and our "Not-I."

The "I," my self, sometimes referred to as the "Ego," is the one with whom I am most familiar. I have a history, a story that began when I was born. Part of this history I remember, but most seems to be forgotten. When we consider the "I", we realize that one part is authentic. "I" am real when my "yes" means yes, my "no" means no. "I" am authentic when I experience and feel the real emotions and feelings that surge within me. "I" am authentic when I experience existential guilt: guilt which arises from having diminished or victimized others and/or myself. "I" am authentic when I am in touch with my living and dynamic faith, hope, and love. "I" am authentic when my activities arise from a free and centered place within. My authentic "I" remembers myself.

But we become aware of much that is not authentic. It is borrowed. "I" am unreal when my "yes" really means no, my "no" often means yes. "I" am inauthentic when I don't remember myself, as if I have no history. "I" am inauthentic when I show secondary emotions and feelings. When we judge our real feeling or emotion is unacceptable, we substitute another that is more acceptable in our culture or to our self-image. These secondary emotions hide the way we really feel. For example, we may show anger rather than fear, because we do not like to show the weakness that fear conveys.

"I" am inauthentic when my activities arise compulsively from my idealized image of myself or from the expectations of others. These are situations in which I wear a mask, play a role, or use protective coverings. We even show secondary feelings and emotions that come from the expectations of our profession. We may display the feelings and emotions that are expected of a doctor, minister, or counselor without really having those feelings and emotions. "I" am inauthentic when I experience super-ego guilt: guilt which does not consider the other person or oneself, but arises from not living up to the Law, to my expectations of myself, or of others. I expect punishment. When I realize that my faith, hope, and love are hand-me-downs and untested, I find that I have not been authentic.

The inauthentic "I" is a secondhand self. Our "inauthentic I" suppresses true feelings, emotions, actions, and guilt: it tries to unseat the true "I" and confuses us.

In addition to the split within the "I" between the authentic and inauthentic, we discover a deeper level within us. We discover an inner stranger, the "Not-I", that we have come to call our unconscious. Our "Not-I" gives hints of itself in excessive emotional reactions, obsessive thoughts, or dreams that may haunt us. It also manifests itself in our inspirations and creativity that seem to carry us beyond ourselves. Our unconscious carries a dynamic living energy as it strives to be born into light out of darkness.

The "Not-I" has different dynamic energies: the Repressed and the Not-Yet. The Repressed is the burial ground for those in ourselves whom we have judged unacceptable. These are the child, adolescent, and young person whose experiences were embarrassing, shameful, or not good enough, not up to our standards. These experiences did not meet our expectations or measure up to what others expected. We have not just forgotten those parts of us. We have driven them into exile. We have dismembered them by cutting them off, banishing them, and pushing them down. We divert much of our life energy to keep these parts of us hidden. We become panicky when they threaten to break out and expose us. These are the parts of ourselves that we can call, using the names coined by the prophets, "forsaken" (Is 62:4), "unloved," and "no-people-of-mine" (Hos 1:6–8).

The Repressed in us are striving to be remembered. They are still alive in us waiting to be accepted, to belong, to be loved. They carry much of our real truth and energy.

They are our Holy Innocents slain before their time, but loved by God. They hold a hidden treasure.

The other dynamic energy seeking to be born, to become incarnate and enfleshed is the Not-Yet. This is the hidden self that Saint Paul assures us must grow strong if we would experience God. This is the inner word of God whom God created in speaking us into existence. Just as Jesus of Nazareth is THE WORD of God, each of us is a word of God. This word of God "is something alive and active" (Heb 4:12). This hidden self, so named by Saint Paul, has been called by different names. It is the "word" of God that we need to speak, the inner "light" of God that we must shine in the darkness; the inner "seed" that God desires to become fertile and fruitful in order to bring God to men and women and men and women to God. This is the *imago Dei*, "image" of God, a word coined by the early fathers of the church. They taught that we were created in the image and likeness of God. Through the effects of original sin, we kept the image but lost our likeness to God. The image of God that we were created to be receded and became hidden within us.

Such is the dynamism of the "Not-I," the unconscious, that we come to understand through our experience. Much energy reserved in both the Repressed and the Not-Yet seeks to enhance us with fuller life. All that we hid by repression and rejection lives together with the word of God hidden within. We might surmise that when we banished these unacceptable parts of ourselves, our inner word of God welcomed them and promised to hold them and to keep them safe until we could accept them. When our word of God appears they also will be liberated. They can join in our chorus to sing "Let all that is within me cry holy."

Both of these energies of the "Not-I" flow together like the tide and undertow, rushing to overwhelm us and drawing us deeper. The Not-Yet urges us to grow strong so we may experience the riches of God and become lovers. We are most like God when we love.

In considering these different aspects of ourselves we find we are a multi-divided person. There is the division between the "I" and the "Not-I"; between the authentic and inauthentic; between the Repressed and the Not-Yet. All these part of ourselves infuse us with dynamic energies. We might compare the unknown land of ourselves to a land with deep inner fissures or tectonic plates that have a continual changing relationship with each other. We have our own interior San Andreas Fault.

Often we desire our hidden self, the inner word of God, to grow strong. But we try to control our interior life for fear the repressed parts will be revealed. We decide who should grow and who should remain hidden. However, the inner word of God, the one who accepts and loves the repressed ones, can find voice only when we have the courage to allow ourselves to know and befriend these lost ones, our own orphans.

At mid-life through the affective changes of conversion, we are led within so that the authentic can mature, the inauthentic can be unmasked, and the Repressed and Not-Yet can be remembered and freed from inner darkness. Then, re-owned, our Word can find its voice; the Seed can unfold; the Light can shine; our hidden self can manifest that God again is present on earth through us.

Saint John of the Cross, following Saint Paul's exhortation, stresses the necessity of growing from a childish relationship with God to that of a mature adult. God wants us to grow from being a child of God to a son or daughter. Perhaps G. K. Chesterton best expresses how we experience this desire in very realistic, concrete terms. In a letter to Monsignor Ronald Knox, he writes:

> I am not troubled about a great fat man who appears on platforms and in caricatures, even when he enjoys controversies on what I believe to be the right side. I am concerned about what has become of a little boy whose father showed him a toy theater, and a schoolboy whom nobody ever heard of, with his brooding on doubts and dirt and day-dreams of crude conscientiousness so inconsistent as to be near to hypocrisy; and all the morbid life of the lonely mind of a living person with whom I have lived. It is that story, that so often came near to ending badly, that I want to end well. Forgive this scrawl, I think you will understand me (pp. 207–8).

As we begin to pay passionate attention to ourselves we discover parts of ourselves who seem like strangers to us but who, in some way, belong to us. They seem to recognize and know us more than we know ourselves. They dissociate and "trick" us from claiming ourselves because we do not acknowledge them as part, albeit unruly and untamed, of ourselves. As we begin the journey into our story, we experience a natural fright.

Teilhard de Chardin writes a graphic description of the fear caused by such a journey.

> For the first time in my life I took a lamp and, leaving the zone of everyday occupations and relationships where everything seems

clear, I went down into my inmost self, to the abyss whence I feel dimly that my power of action emanates. But as I moved further and further away from the conventional certainties by which social life is superficially illuminated, I became aware that I was losing contact with myself. At each step of the descent a new person was disclosed within me of whose name I was no longer sure, and who no longer obeyed me. . . .

At that moment, as anyone else will find who cares to make this same interior experiment, I felt the distress characteristic to a particle adrift in the universe, the distress which makes human wills founder daily under the crushing number of living things and of stars. And if something saved me, it was hearing the voice of the Gospel, guaranteed by divine successes, speaking to me from the depth of the night: *Ego sum, noli timere* (It is I, be not afraid).

Yes, O God, I believe it: and I believe it all the more willingly because it is not only a question of my being consoled, but of my being completed (pp. 76–78).

Through this descent, the Spirit leads us to a new, true foundation within ourselves. The Spirit does not deny or reject any of our efforts, even our sins. The Spirit is the divine potter who continually reshapes, reforms, remolds the material God infused into us. He does not reject it, nor should we. However, we are led into the bottomless abyss to reach this new foundation. We contact primitive aspects in ourselves which, touched by the evil of original sin, we tend to see as monstrous and irrational.

These experiences of the dynamics of conversion that assail us at mid-life have been familiar to men and women in every age. In their efforts to understand themselves and to teach and guide others, they have all stressed the beginning step in this process of conversion. The first phase that is very close to us, on our mouth and in our hearts, is self-knowledge. Using Saint Augustine's image for the spiritual ascent as an edifice, the foundation of which is the humility of self-knowledge and the summit the vision of God, John of the Cross points out the close relationship between our own self-knowledge and our knowledge of God. He quotes Saint Augustine's famous dictum: "Let me know myself, Lord, that I may know you" (Sermo 69, i, 2).

John Maddux claims that Saint Bernard described the pathway of our progress to experience God as one that passes through three levels of truth. The first level begins with coming to know ourselves. This knowledge deepens when we begin to recognize ourselves in our neighbor. Lastly we arrive at the ecstatic knowledge of God in Jesus. Most of us, hoping to experience God, tend to turn our backs on our past and look outside ourselves with great expectations. We are stopped cold when we are told to look inward. All mystics assure us that we must begin by knowing the truth of ourselves. Saint Bernard insists that "the act of turning inward is the first stage of movement outward." He explains this paradox in his treatise "On the Steps of Humility" (Ibid., p. 230).

Self-knowledge is the first step in the movement upward, the initial purification that prepares us for the vision of God. We need to be aware of the trials in our lives, of our misery and sufferings, wounds and sins, truths and lies, and the poverty and richness to be found there. Clement of Alexandria tells us how difficult that is. "Therefore it is the greatest of all disciplines to know oneself; for when a man knows himself, he knows God" (qtd. in R. Johnson, p. 194). In this intimate knowledge of ourselves, we learn true and life giving humility. Saint Teresa of Avila uses similar imagery in *The Interior Castle*. She, too, claims we must begin with the humility of self-knowledge.

When we recollect our experiences during the beginning of conversion, we see they have already introduced us to this first stage of our movement toward God. When the knowledge of ourselves gained through these experiences touches us, we are well aware that we are led to true humility. We find ourselves mired in earth. Filled with dust and ashes, we cry out with Job.

As we grow in self-knowledge, Saint Bernard assures us that when the awareness of our personal misery reaches its deepest point, it is transformed into compassion. We realize our communion with all men and women. "From the first level of truth we pass directly, inevitably, into the second, the truth of others. Aware of our misery, we realize that all share in this condition. All are liars (Ps 115:11): all are wretched and incapable of saving themselves" (Maddux, p. 231).

This occurs when we experience, not just read about, the truth of others in their wounds and sins. We also become aware of their deep desires for healing, freedom, and life. This is especially true of those whom we marginalize, and distance from ourselves. We load them with our projections of what we find unacceptable. We are all one. We are like them and they are like us. We perhaps think we are alone or different. As people tell their stories, we begin to hear stories of hopes, struggles, and failures that are like our own. This helps us to purify our prejudices and intolerance toward those who are different from us in any way.

This awareness leads to the *ecstatic knowledge of God* in Jesus of Nazareth. As we begin to know, *connaître* (i.e., to be born with), Jesus of Nazareth in our own experience, especially in the desert of our own misery as well as on the challenging mountain experiences, we recognize Jesus of Nazareth is Lord and God. He takes us to the Father and the Spirit in the intimacy of love. He is the *way*, the *truth*, the *life!* Just as only in the desert he discovered his way of faithfulness, so the apostles and we discover him in the desert of our experience.

After sharing these dynamics of death and dying with you in this book, I hope to track our progressive pathway to God in future books. I will consider the passages that God leads us through. May God bless and love you.

REFERENCES

Preface

Roberto Assagioli, *Psychosynthesis*, Viking Press, New York, 1965, p. 39.

Introduction

C. G. Jung, *Modern Man in Search of a Soul*, W. S. Dell & Cary F. Baynes, trans., Harvest/HBJ Book, New York, 1933.

Sam Keen, *The Passionate Life: Stages of Loving*, Harper & Row, San Francisco, 1983.

Miriam Greenspan, *Healing Through the Dark Emotions: The Wisdom of Grief, Fear, and Despair*, Shambala, Boston, 2004.

Sydney J. Harris, "Sadly, too few of us grow as we grow older," *Chicago Sun-Times*, date unknown.

Chapter 1

Margery Kempe and others, "A much-needed letter on moderation in spiritual impulses," in *The Cell of Self-knowledge*, adapted and translated by Charles Crawford, Crossroad Publishing Co., New York, 1981.

Rosemary Haughton, *The Passionate God*, Paulist Press, New York, 1981.

Chapter 2

Henri J. M. Nouwen, "Looking into the Fugitive's Eyes," *The Wounded Healer: Ministry in Contemporary Society*, Doubleday, New York, 1972.

Evelyn Underhill, *The House of the Soul*, The Seabury Press, Minneapolis, MN, 1947.

Chapter 3

Barnabas Ahern, "Maturity: Christian Perfection," *The Way*, Supplement 15, Spring 1972.

John Henry Cardinal Newman, *An Essay on the Development of Christian Doctrine*. New edition by C. F. Harrold, Longmans, Green and Co., New York, 1949, p. 38.

"On the Church in the Modern World," *The Documents of Vatican II*, Walter M. Abbott, S.J., gen. ed., America Press, New York, #22, 1966.

Saint Irenaeus, *Adversus hereses*, 3, 18, 7.

Jean Danielou, S.J., "Adam and Christ in St. Irenaeus," *From Shadows to Reality: Studies in the Biblical Typology of the Fathers*, The Newman Press, Westminster, MD, 1960.

Teillard de Chardin, *Hymn of the Universe*, Harper & Row, New York, 1965.

Chapter 4

Gabriel Moran, Homo Viator: An Introduction to a Metaphysic of Hope, Emma Crawford, trans., New York, Harper Torchbooks, 1962.

James Baldwin, *Nobody Knows My Name*, Introduction. Vintage Books, New York, 1993.

Rollo May, *Love and Will*, W. W. Norton Co., New York, 1969.

Chapter 5

Thomas Merton, *The New Man*, Farrar, Straus & Giroux, New York, 1961.

Rollo May, "Contributions of Existential Psychotherapy," in *Existence, A New Dimension in Psychiatry and Psychology*, Rollo May. Ernest Angel, Henri F. Ellenberger, eds., Basic Books, Inc., New York, 1958.

Sam Keen, *The Passionate Life: Stages of Loving*, Harper and Row, San Francisco, 1983.

Thomas P. Malone, M.D. and Patrick T. Malone, M.D., Ph.D., *The Windows of Experience: Experiential Psychology and the Emergent Self*, Simon and Schuster, New York, 1992.

Elisabeth Kübler-Ross, *On Death and Dying*, Scribner Classics, New York, 1969.

Carl G. Jung, *Collected Works*, Vol. 2 R. F. C. Hull, trans., Bollingen Series, Princeton University, 1965.

Frances Vaughan Clark, "Transpersonal Perspectives in Psychotherapy," *Journal of Humanistic Psychology*, Vol. 17, No 2, Spring 1977.

Chapter 6

Thomas Merton, *The New Man*, Farrer, Straus & Giroux, New York, 1961.

Elisabeth Kübler-Ross, *On Death and Dying*, Scribner Classics, New York, 1969.

Gabriel Moran, Homo Viator: An Introduction to a Metaphysic of Hope, Emma Crawford, trans., New York, Harper Torchbooks, 1962.

Evelyn Underhill, *The House of the Soul*, The Seabury Press, Minneapolis, MN, 1947.

Brother David Steindl-Rast, *Gratefulness, the Heart of Prayer*, Paulist Press, Ramsey, NJ, 1984.

Rollo May, *Love and Will*, W. W. Norton Co., New York, 1969.

Chapter 7

The Jerusalem Bible, "Note c for Chapter 42," Alexander Jones, gen. ed., Darton, Longman & Todd, London, 1966.

Louis Evely, *Suffering*, Marie-Claude Thompson, trans., Herder and Herder, New York, 1967.

Takashi Nagai, 1948. Source unknown.

Chapter 8

E. Waugh, *Monsignor Ronald Knox*, Little, Brown and Co., Boston, 1959.

Pierre Teilhard de Chardin, *The Divine Milieu*, Harper Torchbooks, New York, 1965.

Saint Augustine, Sermo 69, i, 2 – ii,3 (PL 38, 441) in *The Collected works of John of the Cross*, trans. Kieran Kavanaugh, O.C.D. & Otilio Rodriguez, O.C.D. Washington, D.C., ICS Publications, 1973.

John S. Maddux, "When You Pray: Self-Knowledge and Prayer," *The Way*, XVII, #3, July 1977.

Clement of Alexandria, quoted in Robert A. Johnson, *WE*, Harper & Row, San Francisco, 1983.

Paul Robb received his Ph.D. in psychology from Loyola University in Chicago, where he taught for a few years. Robb then became the Director of Novices for the Chicago Province of the Society of Jesus. Following that he became a professor of spirituality and ministry at the Jesuit School of Theology in Chicago.

In 1971 he founded the Institute for Spiritual Leadership in Chicago. The Institute sponsored a nine-month program for the education of spiritual directors that was international and ecumenical. It focused on the study of the ways God intervenes in our lives, aids toward self-knowledge, and the art and skills of spiritual direction. The students, all over 35 years of age, were men and women, lay and religious. Robb's nine-month course addressed the dynamics and process of conversion at midlife.

This is his first book.

Summoned at Every Age
Finding God in Our Later Years
Peter van Breemen, S.J.

A book in the **Ignatian Impulse Series**

Aging is indeed a grace. But it is also a multifaceted and complex task. This engaging and easy-to-read book will help readers experience both harmony and fruitfulness during this sometimes-difficult stage of their lives. Ignatius of Loyola made God's desire to give us his very self the foundation of his spirituality. In the same way, van Breemen helps us appreciate that this same gift lies before us as we grow older.

ISBN: 1-59471-036-8 / 128 pages / $9.95

The Circle of Life
The Heart's Journey Through the Seasons
Joyce Rupp and Macrina Wiederkehr
Artwork by Mary Southard

Reflections, poems, prayers, and meditations help us to explore the relationship between the seasons of the earth and the seasons of our lives. Discover the seasons as stepping-stones along the path of the great circle of life, and guides for life's journey.

ISBN: 1-893732-82-7 / 288 pages / $19.95
SORIN BOOKS

Seeds Of Sensitivity
Deepening Your Spiritual Life
Robert Wicks

Wicks leads us on the path of sensitivity, encouraging us not to withdraw from the darkness in our worlds and hearts, while warning us of the pitfalls of cynicism and burnout. Wicks invites us to make a threefold commitment to sensitivity: to self, to others, and to God. *Seeds of Sensitivity* is indeed a guiding light for those seeking to live a sensitive life.

ISBN: 0-87793-541-6 / 160 pages / $9.95

KEYCODE: F0T01050000